ON CREATING
(AND CELEBRATING!)
CHARACTERS

A Science Fiction Writer's Quest
for Characters That Matter

SKYFOX
PUBLISHING

RON COLLINS

On Creating (And Celebrating!) Characters

Cover Design
© Ron Collins
Cover Art: yogysic
A silhouette style vector illustration of
a group of superheroes with light beam effect

Skyfox Publishing

Paperback ISBN-10: 1-946176-58-3
Hardcover ISBN-10: 1-946176-59-1

Paperback ISBN-13: 978-1-946176-58-5
Hardcover ISBN-13: 978-1-946176-59-2

Contents

Acknowledgments

Not to get too far out there, but I would like to thank every writer of every story I've ever read. How's that for casting a wide net?

Perhaps you think this is going too far, but I'm actually serious. The struggle to create great characters is just that, a struggle. And a writer creates them only after the right mix of talent, skill, experience, insight, and understanding come together to make this magical amalgam that makes them happen. Without these struggles, there are no characters. And without these writers there are no struggles.

So, if you are a writer, thank you.

I would also like to thank Lisa Silverthorne, a writer friend of mine whose passion has helped me on my path as a writer.

And, finally, I would like to thank my sweetie, my wife, and forever partner, Lisa. She's the one that created my path in the first place, cleared the way through her patience and support, and — of course — with her immensely skilled copyeditor's gaze.

These days she's my last reader, but she'll always be my first everything else.

Kickstarter Backers

Thank You So Much!

This book owes its origin to these amazing backers!

PunkARTchick *Ruthenia* - A - Erin A. - Marie Andreas - Alex Blackstone - J. A. Bouma -Raphael Bressel - Rebecca Buchanan - Nijeara "Ny" Buie - Michael A. Burstein - Z.J. Cannon - Thorn Coyle - Randy D. – Daizee - Diana Deverell - Justin Dorsey - Laura Rainbow Dragon - Viannah E. Duncan - Raymund Eich - Bonnie Elizabeth - Mason Engel - Charlotte E. English - Jonathan Fesmire - Jerrie the filkferengi - Cora Foerstner - N. Karen Fonville - Andy F - Pierino Gattei – Jim Gotaas - Charlie Grayson - Martin Greening - Jim Henderson - David H. Hendrickson - Eva Holmquist - Jonathan Hudson - J.R. Johnson - Chris Kaiser - Kari Kilgore - Michael Kingswood - Stephen Kotowych - Mark Leslie Lefebvre – Louisa - T. Lovetree - Keith Mackay - Céline Malgen - Adrian McCloskey - Meyari McFarland - Stefon Mears - Ronald H. Miller - Deb Miller - David Neth - Linda Niehoff - C. Nilsson - Lisa Owen - James Palmer - E. R. Paskey - Dwayne Plain - Joseph Procopio - Emilia Pulliainen - Mary Jo Rabe - Annie Reed - Matthea W. Ross - Johanna Rothman - Shadowfall - Martin L. Shoemaker - Shawn Shultz - Dillon Sim - Dean Wesley Smith - Steven M. Smith - Carolyn Ivy Stein - Stephannie Tallent   Rob Vagle - Greg Vose - Laura Ware - Kelly Washington - Keith West, Future Potentate of the Solar System - Ryan M. Williams - Danielle Williams - Filip Wiltgren – Sean Young - Dr.ZeroStone

For Readers Who Love People Who Do Not Technically Exist

Celebrating Characters
Story Is Character,
and Character Is Story

LET'S talk about what makes people real.

That's what my favorite characters are to me. Real. If you're reading this, I suspect that's what they are to you, too.

Characters I love often feel as real to me as people I know in the physical world. Whether from books, movies, comics, television shows, or any other form of entertainment, the characters I love mean something to me. They give me hope. They teach me lessons that become ingrained into the fabric that makes me who I am.

As you'll soon discover, if you get me spun up, I can talk about my favorite characters in the same way I talk about best friends.

So, yes. The characters I love are real to me, and there isn't anything you can do or say to convince me otherwise.

If you're the same way, this book is for you.

I THINK it's fair to say that marvelous characters I find in books are even more special than those I come across in more visual formats, because—since these characters exist only in my mind— they become at least partially personal. Whereas a hero of mine in the Real World belongs to everyone, I am free to envision characters in books however I want.

My Sherlock Holmes is different from yours, right? I came

across him differently than you did, and I built my understanding of him on my own.

You are, of course, free to have your own Holmes.

That's the beauty of great characters, particularly in books: They live in a multiverse constrained only by the size of humanity itself.

Great characters matter to us.

We can create metaphors around great characters—meaning that, like any celebrity, a well-written character can be a spectacular source of gossip—which is something else we humans like to do. *Did you see the look [insert favorite character from your favorite show here] gave him, when [insert your favorite heartthrob here] walked into the room? If they're not together by next week, I'm gonna throw a chair through the screen.*

I once heard Paul Simon talking about his song "Mrs. Robinson," in which he asks the famous question about where Joe DiMaggio has gone. As I recall, Simon reported that the literal-minded DiMaggio wasn't particularly happy with the reference, suggesting he hadn't gone anywhere. "I guess Joe wasn't comfortable being a metaphor," Simon said.

Yet, metaphor he was. Simply because his celebrity turned the persona he portrayed to the public into the form of a character. Real, but not real.

There's Michael Jordan and there's Michael Jordan the person. Unless we are a friend of his, all we get is the metaphor (cue Jordan's "And I took that personally" meme).

WHAT DOES it mean to celebrate characters?

Well?

That's an interesting question. I've asked it of myself often while putting this book together.

That's what happens when I flash on a title and think *hey, that sounds like fun,* and then find myself having to write it. I tend to overthink these things, you know? I give an off-the-cuff answer, then argue with myself.

Yes, it's fun to be inside my head.

I don't think I'm alone in this matter, though.

Describing exactly why we love the characters we love can be hard to grapple with. People are complex and weird. But we will try. And in the end, we'll get the job done.

That's a form of celebration.

We love these characters for who they are and how they make us feel.

You'll find some of that in this book.

Writers, of course, talk about characters all the time—at least when we're not talking business. At first, I didn't consider that discussion to be a form of celebration so much as a vivisection. On the other hand, medical folks love learning how the body works, so what do I know?

And writers do what they do to learn about characters. We go to workshops to share tips and ideas. We read. We mimic. We listen to podcasts. We think about such dry things as the value and purpose of characters in stories—though we don't put it that way all the time.

Recently, for example, I saw David B. Coe, a friend who has provided blurbs for my work, posted advice about characters—specifically how to change the dynamic of established ensembles by inserting new ones into your work. In this case, he examined what happened when *Star Trek: The Next Generation* inserted Ro Laren (a Bajoran rebel turned Starfleet officer) into the mix, when *Buffy the Vampire Slayer* added the morally ambiguous Faith Lehane, and when southern Republican Ainsley Hayes joined *The West Wing*.

Each of these, he said, spiced up the mix and added new complexities for stories that couldn't exist without their new blood.

I think he's spot-on.

In the end, this examination counts as a form of celebration. The desire to know everything about another person is a sincere form of flattery, right?

As you might guess, there will be a lot of this type of celebration in this book, too.

Then there are the more ephemeral aspects of our celebrations. The way we keep characters on the edges of our existence, using them to leverage more ideas.

This is the area of the subconscious.

The act of incorporating these characters into the fabric of who we are.

We—both writers and readers—dream about characters. Sometimes so much so that, as my friend Lisa Silverthorne relates about her most recent series, she wakes up at three o'clock in the morning with her characters demanding three new books.

Speaking for myself, I sometimes model characters off real people, mixing and matching parts, grafting them together to make my own Frankenstein's monster. One of my favorite short stories features a character who is an amalgam of multiple members of my family. In this fashion, that character is a ghostly golem that came from nowhere.

That aspect of generation—how characters are born—is another form of celebration.

Do they jump whole cloth from my imagination? Did I draw them up in character sheets?

I've heard writers say they interview their characters before they put them on the page. I've heard of others who write letters from their characters' points of view. Years back, I ran across a writer who pasted images of people they found intriguing into notebooks so they could use them to inspire characters.

The ideas are infinite, and no path is wrong.

Sharing origin stories is a form of celebration, though, right?

You'll find touches of that spice in the mix here, too.

REGARDLESS OF HOW writers square the corners, the goal is the same. We want to create characters that readers love and remember.

We want to create characters that matter.

As a pragmatic matter, creating these interesting, well-rounded, and believable characters is an essential aspect of writing good fiction. But beyond that, it's just flat-out fun. Great characters are the lifeblood of any story because great characters are what make stories memorable—both the reading and the writing thereof.

We become emotionally invested in characters that matter because they make stories engaging. We love them because they help us step away from our own lives for just those few moments. Sherlock Holmes and Dr. Watson. John Wick. Harley Quinn. Jack Reacher. Katniss Everdeen. John McClane. Lizbeth Salander. Jo, Meg, Amy, and Beth. These characters are bigger than life. Even if you haven't read the books these people come from, it's likely their names put images into your head.

We are all human beings, after all—at least until our AI over-lords finish their arrival (next Tuesday, maybe?). We like to daydream. Great, engaging characters help us to live in other shoes.

THE CHALLENGE, of course, is how to make characters that readers will remember.

Which is why I'm here now.

I'm writing this little book because, well, I'm the teensiest bit analytical (cue all my friends laughing at the term *teensiest bit*), and because I want to talk about what characters mean to me.

Why are these characters important?

How do they come about when I'm writing?

Why do they matter when I'm reading?

Though I'll be sprinkling in a bit of advice here and there, this isn't meant as a cold, *how-to* manual so much as a celebratory *why-to* gathering of characters I consider great fun.

But, of course, if a writer, or a reader for that matter, grasps the *why* of it all, then the recursive magic of *how* kicks in that much more fully.

Don't ask me why it works that way but trust me when I say it does. Life is full of tricky bits like that, and I figure if you get to the point where you understand completely how that works, then it just wouldn't be fun anymore.

So that's what I'll be doing in this celebration of great characters.

Among other things, I'll be talking about why I love various characters and what I'm thinking about as I go about my toils in trying to create my own.

Along the way, I'll be defining myself just a bit, too. Because that's another thing about the characters we love. Our fandom helps define our identities. The kinds of characters we love tell the world who we are.

It will be a partial picture, though.

I say that because, so that this book can appeal to the widest audience I can reach, I've chosen to examine characters drawn from stories that are widely known. That makes sense, right? I want you, my reader, to be able to relate to these characters, so I'll not spend time on hundreds of characters I also love, but who appeared in smaller, niche publications.

I'll not talk about Irette Patterson's Ben, for example.

Nor Lisa Silverthorne's Bode Jameson.

It also means I'll pull from multiple forms of media. Movies and television as well as books.

All I can promise is that every character I mention (and there will be quite a cast) is someone I love in one fashion or another.

I hope you love them, too, of course.

If you love the same characters I do, that's wonderful!

But it will be even better if something you read here makes you see your own list of loves in different and deeper ways.

That's a form of celebration too, isn't it?

If you like reading about, talking about, and thinking about your favorite characters in ways you haven't before, I think you'll like reading this book.

I know I've loved writing it.

Believable vs. Real?
Reader Perspectives

It is a truth universally acknowledged, that we know great characters when we read them.

Great characters jump off the page, don't they? Well … except for the ones who, rather than take such an aggressive approach, slowly work their way under our skin. Or the ones who hang around as wallflowers until suddenly we see them for who they really are and want to hug them into us and never let go.

It's complicated.

Creating characters who jump off the page is not easy.

When you're writing, making a great character can be mind-numbingly frustrating. Being the writer, you feel like you know these characters inside and out, but you also see that what's spilling onto the page isn't cutting it. That realization is followed immediately by a stultifying wave of omnipresent powerlessness that threatens to grind you to a pulp.

What do you do?

Tweak here or there? Cut that chunk of exposition? Scatter in new bits?

Scrap the whole thing and redraft?

The fight is real.

Let's start by thinking about the difference between *believable* and *real*.

To see what I mean, let me consider a high-profile pop star

I've never met—I'll call her Taylor Swift—and my friend who plays guitar in a bar down the road.

Taylor Swift is believable.

My friend is real.

Setting aside that Taylor Swift is an actual, real person who most definitely exists in our world, and that her publicly presented antics are there for me to see, the truth is that, beyond her business persona, I don't know anything about her. I like her vibe, but given my lack of any relationship with her, her presence is not deep for me. Sure, Taylor Swift's celebrity allows me to *pretend* I know her, but I have no idea if my picture of her is true. And unless I make up my own version of Taylor Swift (which is not what I come to a story for), I don't have a deep enough framework to know how to feel when presented with how she deals with problems.

As a reader, if your story presents me characters at what I feel as Taylor Swift distances—even if they are believable—I'm not going to connect with them.

I need something closer to my bones. I need you to draw me into your Taylor Swift doppelganger by giving me something more intimate than what I see in her public persona.

It is logical, then, that my friend playing guitar down the street feels more real to me. I've spent time with him, right? I've seen him react to situations that I haven't even seen Taylor Swift in.

So, yes, while the semantic difference between the words *believable* and *real* can be fun to discuss, I'm suggesting that the difference is both real and important.

I say that because of my own *reading* experience.

As a reader, the deal I make when I crack open your new book is that I will give you, the writer, the benefit of the doubt—

that I will begin the story believing the places, events, and characters in that book exist. I will, in fact, assume your characters and settings are important because otherwise you wouldn't be introducing them to me.

This makes sense, doesn't it?

It takes a certain kind of dedicated masochist to pick up a book while actively wanting to hate it, and last I checked, I'm not that kind of masochist.*

As a reader, I'm on your side.

I want to be entertained.

I am ready to be led, so I'll give you time to prove that, yes, those characters belong on the page, and if you do that, and begin to move me to the point where the characters are deep enough that I feel like I know them, I'll buy them hook, line, and sinker.

That's your job.

Give me what I need to eventually see your characters—and especially your main cast—as more than simply believable, and I'm there for you.

This means that every character a writer introduces to me, be they The Great Gatsby, Jane Eyre, or Aladdin's Djinni, springs instantly to life inside my head as *believable*. This happens even though they all begin as literally nothing but squiggles on a page.

There are limits to my patience, though, so hopefully, progress will be quick.

So, respect my patience as I'm reading along.

Get to work.

First page, even. Or first sentence.

That's the goal, anyway.

Great first sentences (and great first paragraphs, sections, and chapters), even when they don't say something specifically about a character, say something about the characters in that story. And making your characters jump from being simply believable to being actually real, as quickly as possible, is a fantastic way to hook a reader.

HERE IS an exercise you can do on your own that might help you.

Go to your favorite bookseller's list of current top sellers. Pick three categories at random and open the top seller in each category. Read the first sentence. Ask yourself, after reading only that sentence, what the writer has given you about the character.

I did this today, selecting Thrillers, Romance, and Fantasy.

Here is my result:

THRILLER: *Laura Dave – The Last Thing He Told Me*

OWEN USED to like to tease me about how I lose everything, about how, in my own way, I have raised losing things to an art form.

ROMANCE: *Pippa Grant – The Worst Wedding Date*

I DIDN'T KNOW *bridesmaid* was code for *babysitter for the bride's brother*, but if that's what my best friend needs of me for her dream wedding to go off without a hitch, that's what I'll do.

FANTASY: *Carissa Broadbent – The Ashes and the Star-Cursed King*

THE KING KNEW, in this moment, that his greatest love would also be his ruination, and that both would come in the unlikely form of a young human woman.

· · ·

Spiffy, right?

Reading opening lines is a classic exercise, but one of the things I love about this form of it is that it lets a writer understand how similar storytelling is across genres.

Because bestseller lists change often, your results will be different from mine.

The learning will be the same, though.

So, anyway, how do we do that?

How do we make characters real to our loyal readers?

The answer to that question is certainly bigger than simply crafting hooky first lines. It's a question that needs more than a one-line answer—more than a paragraph or even a chapter. The answer is hard to come by, though, because everything counts.

Every event, every reaction, every piece of dialog, every movement—even the tiny nuances of how a character adjusts to things around them—becomes a decision point for readers.

Is that character still believable? Did their reaction to that problem feel right? Did I enjoy that? Was it fun? Was it worrisome?

Is that interesting?

My grandfather, who was a solid country-boy fisherman in his heart, would tell stories about the wide gap between hooking a fish and reeling them in. The same thing exists for us writers. Hooking a reader is good—but the game is still afoot until we land the story. If we're not diligent in our efforts, we can lose a reader at any time.

The reader is on our side, though.

Each step of the way adds trust.

The problem is that readers are sometimes difficult to understand.

Readers are weird, see?

Readers are people, and people are complex.

So, I'm going to spend the rest of this book talking about the wide range of tools I use to gather readers' interests, or—to be proper with my attributions—the wide range of tools I've seen others use, and that I've tried to form into my own toolbox.

Scanning the Table of Contents of this book shows you it's a big toolbox.

** FUN ASIDE: an interesting rule of thumb says readers are looking for any way into a story, whereas editors are looking for any way out of it. This makes sense. An editor can publish only a small amount of what they receive. Therefore, the editor's job is to reject 95% or more of the manuscripts that hit what they lovingly call their slush pile. Their goal is to spend as little time as possible culling the herd. So, reading like an editor means actively looking for reasons to stop reading. Readers, however, are exactly the opposite. Readers begin hoping they will love a story. They came to my book because they want me to entertain them. So, if I give them something good, they'll take it, internalize it, and make it their own.*

First Impressions & Mission Statements
Gandalf the Grey

JUST LIKE REAL PEOPLE, first impressions matter.

Think about the last book you read (before this one!) or your favorite show of the moment.

Imagine your favorite character.

What do you remember of their first scene?

Is it still blisteringly clear to you? Or is it hazy in the way you remember an old picture? Either way, if you go back and take in that scene again, I'm willing to bet you'll be amazed at the information the writer presented to you at that moment.

Characters become interesting when they react to the world around them in ways that make sense. They become real when those things firm up into a thicker paste. The way characters think and react tells us what the character sees as important, you see. The things they notice, and the way they describe them defines so much about them.

So, when a writer introduces me to a character, they are giving me a baseline for what that character is all about. It's that baseline that will let that character drive the story forward. In that sense, the entry point of every character becomes the foundation from which I will judge that character's behavior from that time forward.

Once the foundation is set, if the character strays too far from that baseline—at least without an obvious shift in personality or worldview due to story events—I might decide that this character has become unbelievable, and then metaphorically toss said book across said room.

This is bad for the writer.

(And not good for the book, either)

Likewise, if a writer half-asses the character's background from the beginning, then that writer has given me no foundation from which to make judgments. In this case, I'd guess the character won't hold my interest at all.

A solid introduction, though?

Well—a well-made introduction can be sneaky. A well-made introduction can do remarkable things.

Let's look at a brilliant one—specifically, Gandalf the Grey, the *Lord of the Rings*' chief wizard.

When we first meet Gandalf, he makes this statement: "A wizard is never late, Frodo Baggins. Nor is he early. A wizard arrives precisely when he means to."

Do we believe him? Of course, we do.

The line is a bit pretentious but, in the context of his arrival on the scene, and the fact that he is most definitely a high-and-mighty wizard, we believe him completely. Wizards are supposed to be the slightest bit full of themselves. So that works anyway. But there is more going on here than we see at first glance. Gandalf delivers the line in a lighthearted moment, and with a wry essence of humor, but the mysterious layer in its delivery carries an ominous undertone that underlies the whole of what is to come.

It also serves to tell the reader something important about Gandalf

He is secretive. He has intentions.

He is calculating things that—right now—no one else sees.

The first time you experience his introductory line, it simply works. But rereading it allows us to delve deeper into its meanings—which are right there, hidden in plain sight. Gandalf knows something is brewing, and he knows he's going to have a part in it. Gandalf is watching. And he's planning.

A writer could do worse than to study the value of this phrase in that context, because that introduction may well be perfect in its execution relative to its purpose in the story it fills.

The phrase deflects Frodo's query of the moment but is also the truth.

Gandalf has arrived at the shire at this precise moment precisely because he means to be here. And he means to be here for reasons that are quite dire. Though we don't know it yet, with this phrase Gandalf is giving us his mission statement. It's his purpose as a human being. He is working to save the world, and he is going to arrive wherever he arrives precisely because he means to.

Gandalf is more than a wizard, though.

As the story progresses, J.R.R. Tolkien adds layers to Gandalf's foundation, and it all makes sense because of this mission statement he's already delivered.

Gandalf has struggles, both personal and professional. He is wise and knowledgeable, but he is also impatient and prone to let hobbits get away with too much for their own good. All these things make him more real as a person, and as the story progresses, he becomes even more believable as a sorcery-spinning character embedded in what, in the end, is a fantastical Epic Fantasy.

We can believe in the magic Gandalf casts because Gandalf is who he is.

Even if Gandalf makes a mistake, his choices always fall in line with the traits and goals we've seen built from the foundation of that first mission statement.

This is the magic trick the author is trying to pull off.

Gandalf is believable as a sorcerer in a fantasy setting, but he becomes a real, breathing character because his reactions to the problems he's presented always conform to the foundation Tolkien first gave us: "A wizard is never late, Frodo Baggins. Nor is he early. A wizard arrives precisely when he means to."

Beautiful.

First Impressions, Mission Statements, & Secrets

Jack Pearson

ALL RIGHT. Let's keep our focus on introductions but shift the lens just a little. Gandalf comes from a work of magic—which does not exist in our modern world. So, let's look at a more contemporary figure: Jack Pearson from the television series *This Is Us*.

From the get-go, I was a major fan of the show.

The storytelling was sharp. The characters were interesting. The first five episodes—which focused on Randall, Jack's adopted son, and Randall's biological father—were a perfect short story all by itself. I would have been happy if the whole thing had shut down right then.

Thank goodness it didn't, though.

By its end, I loved Jack Pearson fully, completely, and without reservation. But that wasn't always the case. In fact, if there was something I disliked about *This Is Us*, early in its run, it would be wrapped up in a Jack-sized box.

Let me see if I can explain this in writer-speak.

First, for those who didn't watch, the *This Is Us* storyline followed the lives of Jack and Rebecca Pearson, and their three kids across multiple timelines, with each episode focusing on a different member of the family, each of which was a complex character on their own.

While it was running, I loved going to Twitter to see how fans talked about each of the characters.

In the earliest episodes, the father figure—Jack—had his detractors, and of course, I was one.

He was too perfect, you see.

Too loving.

Too much "there" for his kids and his wife.

I mean, the guy walked on water.

No problem was too big or too small for Perfect Jack Pearson to bring his Peter Perfect bravado into.

Turns out Jack Pearson was far from perfect, though. Turns out he had a secret. Turns out Jack came from a deeply troubled household that included an abusive, alcoholic father, and he was a man who was still struggling with that same alcoholism. We all know people with tough origin stories, and it's a cliché to say that people from those backgrounds either fall into perpetuating the chain or somehow find the strength to pull themselves out of the morass to become a much better person than the ones that raised them.

Turns out Jack is type #2.

He is not, he's decided, going to be his father—and that informs everything he does.

All right, then. With that behind us, and in line with what I did with Gandalf, let me take a moment to look at how the writers of *This Is Us* introduced their audience to Jack.

When we first meet him, Jack Pearson is sitting patiently on the edge of his bed, naked except for a yellow, Pittsburgh Steeler terrible towel laid across his delicates—a towel we soon learn is part of his birthday present. He's turning thirty-six. He's waiting for his wife to perform their traditional birthday dance. The problem is that Rebecca, said wife, is hugely pregnant with triplets now, and uncomfortable doing the dance.

"Tradition is tradition," Jack chides, smiling in a perfectly Jack kind of way.

Jack is relatable as hell here. As is Rebecca, for that matter. You can tell they are perfect together—but this essay is about Jack Pearson, so I'll focus on him.

He's completely believable in this introductory moment. We can tell Jack is a happy person.

A moment later, he's leaning over Rebecca's swollen belly, talking directly to his unborn kids, and we're feeling even better about him. We know men like this. If we're fathers, we may well *be* people like this.

Here is what Jack says to his kids at that moment before they are even born: "Hey, Big Three, do you three know how much I love your mother? I mean, do you even have any idea?"

There it is. Just like the Gandalf example, there is Jack Pearson's mission statement laying there as bare as he is under that terrible towel. Though the viewer doesn't know it, for the rest of his life, Jack is going to focus all his effort on making certain his kids and his wife know exactly how much he loves them.

From a story perspective, the right question we should be asking at that point, though, as is the right question throughout most stories, is *why?*

Of course, the writers don't answer that one right away.

Instead, writerly sleight of hand occurs, and things happen to push that "why" question to the side so we can watch Jack deal with a series of intense, short-term problems, always reacting per his mission statement (that, like Gandalf before him, we still don't yet fully see as his mission statement).

The result, in those early episodes—before we get to peek under the hood and discover the wires and chains that drive his dedication—is that Jack can be too much.

He's borderline too perfect to be believed.

Real people don't act that way.

Except, of course, when they do.

Episodes later, as time reveals the depth of his damage, we come to see him as a person who, while certainly loving, is driven as much by the darker sides of human nature as any need to be perfect. As we learn more about Jack, we understand that the saccharine layer of perfection we felt in those early episodes was at least partially a façade. And, as each layer of the façade rolls off, he becomes so solidly real that I, for one, was almost embarrassed to have doubted him.

Since we don't see that secret up front, the reveal of each layer is sometimes incredibly intense.

HERE'S ANOTHER THING, too: That feeling I got about Perfect Jack Pearson at the beginning of the series ends up serving as a boomerang for this effect.

Jack is embarrassed and ashamed of his father.

There's a barrier between him and that feeling, though.

It's a purposeful barrier Jack has built around him, a façade so thick that I don't think he even lets himself feel it unless something comes up that forces him to face it. That façade Jack hides behind *is* an important part of his personality.

As I meet him, though, all I know is that there's an odd relationship between Jack and his devotion to his family. Something isn't quite right, and it makes me a little uncomfortable.

I feel his façade because I'm missing information. That feeling annoyed me at times, but Jack was entertaining enough, and the rest of the storyline was fascinating enough I could power through. As I said, the story arc of Randall and his biological father was deeply moving. That alone helped me to ignore the Jack problem.

Then the writers started peeling away the layers and as the hammer of Jack's truth fell, the fact that I'd sensed that shield as an annoyance hit home.

That shield is due to his problem.

And the writers made me feel it, then used that feeling so subtly that I could have easily missed it.

I'm embarrassed to have doubted Jack—just as Jack was embarrassed by his father.

Brilliant.

Wickedly Effective Introductions
Last Thoughts

I DECIDED to lead off this volume with Gandalf and Jack Pearson because their stories seem so dramatically different, and yet their introductions were so similar when looked at in the context of their stories.

Both introductions show the character as fundamentally a good person. Both give the character's purpose in statements that the writers cloak in the moment.

And both have a secret of sorts.

Gandalf's is a worldly secret, which is one reason *Lord of the Rings* needs to reveal it early in the storyline. Jack's is deeply personal and comes out later in the flow. But both secrets are there in scene one.

In each case, the revelation of these secrets makes the character stronger, in that I find it easier to understand both Gandalf and Jack at that moment. Finally, in both cases, once I understand them, I'm totally on their side.

A writer could always do worse than pay attention to the introduction of the main characters because the main character is almost always going to carry thematic messages.

So read those introductions (or watch them) again.

Do your best to ignore misdirection going on in the foreground and pay attention to what's going on underneath the surface.

Use introductions as the opportunities they are.

Realize that what I see as a reader during an introduction is not all I can get.

Here's another little secret. The moment you are introducing a new character is the moment I (as your reader) am most open to letting you trick me into missing the forest for the trees.

Take advantage of that.

If you're having trouble getting into a character, ask yourself the One Question That Rules Them All.

What is it that drives this character?

THEN GIVE it to us in a cloaked shell.

Hidden in plain sight.

Obvious in retrospect, but so easy to miss.

Do that well, and you'll delight me as a reader.

Personality
Tyrion Lannister

GREAT CHARACTERS COME with deep personalities.

This is something that seems so obvious that I shouldn't need to say it.

Unless, that is, I stop to think about it.

Is that true?

For me, the problem is the word *deep*.

If we think about it, we can all name characters we love who don't go particularly deep. Superman, for example, isn't particularly complex. Clark Kent has more to him, but, even then, he isn't too deep and, to be real here, I don't often need much from the writers of Superman to enjoy the basic plots of his stories.

Then there's this tip that Mike Resnick once gave me about writing robots—who, by definition, don't have personalities at all (yes, even Data in *Star Trek*, who is constantly trying on various ideas but does not have an organic personality beyond the cold logic of his positronic brain). Paraphrasing Mike here, he said that since robots can't feel things, just put them into positions where the reader can feel for them, and things will work out well.

Bottom line: robot stories can be great, and robots have no personality at all.

The question of how important a character's personality is can be related to Mike's lesson, though, because readers want to relate to characters, and the character's personality is a direct window to their worldview. When a writer removes personality from the equation completely, they are hoping to make the reader fill it in for them.

Of course, HAL 9000 is a different kind of beast in *2001: A Space Odyssey*. As is, well, *Jaws*.

I'll get to villains soon enough, though.

But no. It is not a requirement that characters have deep personalities.

All those caveats said, though, for most characters a deep personality helps readers relate. Personality is their frame of reference to the world. It informs everything about how characters react to events. So, deep or not, personalities are important.

Readers want these characters to be their friends, too. And personalities help readers relate to characters. Or, in the case of villains, readers want to understand why villains do their villainous things. Sure, readers can sometimes live with "evil is as evil does," but if you're like me, and if it is true that every character is a hero of their own stories, you prefer to see what part of a villain's personality drives them to do these evil things.

How can the villain sleep at night?

In other words: Hannibal Lecter is different from the Joker. Show me how.

So, if we're good with the idea that a character's personality is important for us writers to think about, let's start with the basics.

Just what is a personality?

Let me start by doing the old dictionary challenge. We love that game, right? So, so fun!

You know where this is going, though.

The Oxford Languages dictionary says that personality is *the combination of characteristics or qualities that form an individual's distinctive character.*

I may not be in good standing to argue with the Oxford Languages dictionary, but to my eye that is a recursive definition if ever there was one.

I humbly suggest that "an individual's distinctive character" is a synonym for their personality. In fact, if I had seen the definition of personality as "an individual's distinctive character," I would have gone with it. Given that, the definition of a personality then is *the combination of characteristics or qualities that form an individual's personality.*

Yeesh.

See?

Recursive.

And don't even start with the use of "characteristics" ... that form ... "character."

Maybe it's just me.

Anyway, the whole thing is quite open-ended, isn't it?

If nothing else, the Oxford Languages definition does help in that, if I relax a little, I can read it to indicate that personality is a (potentially infinite) combination of characteristics and qualities that add up to define that person.

I can live with that.

I ONCE HEARD Mary Doria Russell say that, if you want to know who a person is, find out what their life was like when they were fourteen years old. After that, she argued, they spend the rest of their time dealing with that fourteen-year-old inside them.

I'm not certain that's true all the time, but it seems like a good place to start. So much of a person's approach to life seems to extend naturally from those early years.

And the literary landscape brims with interesting tests of Russell's idea.

Here's just one.

Tyrion Lannister

OF THE MYRIAD of characters G.R.R. Martin used to populate his *Game of Thrones* masterwork, I'm thinking right now about Tyrion Lannister, played so majestically by Peter Dinklage in the HBO adaptation.

You can count me among the masses of fans.

While the storyline presented was truly epic in all ways, for my time, watching Peter Dinklage bring Tyrion to life was the most exquisite fun. His humor was dry. His wit was searing. Watching his political machinations work out was the definition of delicious.

Yes.

I loved me some Tyrion.

It's fair to say Tyrion Lannister is one of the most complicated and fleshed-out of all the *GoT* characters. I could go further and say that, indeed, Tyrion may well be among the most complex and fleshed-out characters in all of literature.

Tyrion is whip-smart and politically savvy.

He's armed with a keen sense of observation, and a caustic wit that he uses with reckless abandon. He also has intimacy problems. Despite yearning for said intimacy, Tyrion is not comfortable with it, and—in the end—it is this difficulty that gives him such compassion for marginalized and mistreated characters.

Let's ask ourselves why that is.

What did George R.R. Martin—and the writers of *Game of Thrones*—do to paint Tyrion with such vivid colors?

First, Tyrion was born a dwarf, so he's physically different from the norm. This means people have been ridiculing and underestimating him his whole life. That sharp wit he carries has come about as a mechanism of self-defense, and as his best way to go on the attack. He has no physical advantage over anyone, but in a war of words, Tyrion Lannister has few peers.

The Lannisters are also a family with extreme power, which means he came into this world with expectations already bestowed upon him. Those expectations have warped his relationship with command and control, as have the inner squabbles of his family's positioning. His sister, Cersei, and his brother, Jaime, are the golden ones. The treatment of his domineering father, who blames Tyrion for the death of his wife—who expired giving birth to Tyrion—has further bent Tyrion's sense of self-worth. As result, Tyrion has never felt like he was a fully functional part of his family.

I argue his powers of observation and political acumen spring from this dynamic, too. Being an underpowered, overwhelmed outsider in his own family, an abused son and brother, Tyrion has had to spend his life witnessing and assessing simply to survive. His intelligence comes from a youth spent constantly adding one and one to get two, finding patterns, and then jumping ahead to three when no one else quite saw things as they were.

While we don't see Tyrion at age fourteen, it's obvious he formed these parts of his personality in his youth. Subsequently, we see them play out in Tyrion's behavior throughout the entire series. Along the way, we get bits and pieces of his background in ways that let us form a full picture as time proceeds.

Early in the series, we interpret Tyrion's frequent visits to brothels as acts of wanton debauchery.

Later we'll be able to understand better how this behavior stems from his status as an outsider and from ostracization by those closest to him. He wants to love these women he visits, and in fact, does fall in love with them at times even as he knows it cannot end well. He's a broken person.

And, yet … the fact that he can find comfort in their arms forms his sense of indebtedness to those downtrodden of the oppressed, working class (cue Simon and Garfunkel's "The Boxer" here.)

Anyway, the bottom line is that any final analysis says that Tyrion is a massively complex personality whose despairingly painful life experiences have dramatically shaped his strengths and weaknesses.

If you believe Mary Doria Russell, and at this point, I see no reason not to, his whole adult life was spent dealing with the person he had become by age fourteen. Whether you buy Russell's concept or not, though, the case of Tyrion Lannister shows there is something to the idea that characters on the page benefit from having deeply formed personalities, and that a writer can do worse than dig into the psychology and personality of their characters as they are growing up.

How Much Background?
Batman & Katniss Everdeen

It's a classic icebreaker because most of us are curious about other people—especially people we're first meeting. We want the inside scoop.

In the last chapter, I argued that most engaging characters come with deep personalities and that deep personalities are often related to the character's background.

But how much background do we need? *(enough)*

Can you have too much? *(yes)*

What happens if we don't get enough? *(disaster, I say! Total disaster!)*

The answer to this basic question is tougher than we'd like to think.

On one hand, you've got writers arguing that we should take out everything that isn't the story, on the other you've got a phalanx of other writers who urge you to make your characters deep and robust, to the point of ignoring all else. If you wrote it, leave it!

It's enough to drive a person insane.

Your mileage can vary, of course.

The decisions a writer makes regarding what background to include, and how to best describe that background goes to define a writer's voice, too, which is a slippery slope on a patch of quicksand if ever there was one.

For me, though, the answer lies in the story itself. By that, I mean that the amount of background a reader needs to cement a character as real to them varies depending on the needs of the story. Main characters, in general, need more, supporting characters less, depending on the decisions and events in the story, anyway. From a mechanical point of view, characters need whatever background is necessary to give them enough believability to sell their reactions to the plot twists we're putting in front of them.

There's also the question of timing.

In the case of each of the characters I've touched on in any depth so far (Gandalf the Grey, Jack Pearson, and Tyrion Lannister), their writers have not just dumped the depths of the character's backgrounds into their manuscripts like so much muck for us readers to wade through. That background is, instead, dribbled out in little pieces of action, reaction, dialog, and other such bits throughout the entire span of the story scape, with just enough provided as we're ready for at the time.

Sometimes the story gives us that background directly from the characters themselves. Jack Pearson, for example, has an entire thread in which the writers show us his and his brother's family life. But he also has moments in "current" timelines in which he conveys stories. Other times we get parts of their stories from side characters. In Jack's case they come from his best friend, and also from his brother.

Remember that when we get to discussing supporting characters. They exist to add depth to the main characters, and telling parts of the main characters' stories through them can be very effective.

Sometimes those stories don't jibe perfectly, and, in the case of Jack, we see that inconsistency as Jack protecting himself in the telling—or protecting his family—which goes to his character.

With each drib and drab, these characters come even more fully to life.

A QUICK ASIDE: Though physicality, orientation, and gender do *influence* background, I'm not considering them as being part of the character's actual background here. Tyrion's dwarfism is an immutable part of him, of course. As is, say, The Hulk's overgrown muscles. But I don't tend to group them directly as background.

Those things make up the "nature" part of a character's basic makeup (versus nurture), so the questions about how much background to include doesn't apply quite as well.

Female, male, trans, non-binary, tall, gawky, person of color … all of these are relevant, so—as the story needs them—they should be there. But for my argument's sake, I'm bucketing those items in the category of a character's physicality rather than their background.

Feel free to disagree!

By background, right now, anyway, I'm talking about things that happened to and around the character that formed that character's basic makeup. In other words, the "nurture" part of the "nature or nurture" question.

So, yes. External forces.

Occupation can fit. Co-workers can influence development. And the character's path to their occupation would count. Why is your best friend a lawyer? Why does your other best friend own an independent boutique? Past life experiences qualify. Failures and successes work because every one of those experiences affected a character's social existence.

Upbringing. Family wealth. Exposure to education.

How much do you need?

The answer is, of course, it depends.

What does it depend on?

The story, naturally.

LET'S look at examples to decide what that might mean.

Batman isn't Batman, for example, without his aloof aura of isolation. At his root, he's a vigilante. So, we need that isolation in the storyline to believe him. His comfort in building the bat cave does wonders here. We also need to see how Bruce Wayne's quest for justice springs from seeing his parents killed, and how his ability to pursue his career as a vigilante comes from the wealth he inherits. But we see Bruce Wayne is intelligent, too, both by how he addresses his vigilante gig as well as how he's quietly turned his family fortune into an even bigger pile.

Batman is fundamentally good at heart—which we get not only from his quest to stop crime but from his relationships with Alfred (his family butler) and characters like Commissioner Gordon and Robin.

I think that's it, though.

When it comes down to it, the key pieces we need to enjoy and understand a Batman story—as with a Superman story—are slimmer than others need. More background can still work, but we don't need it to enjoy one of his stories, so, I argue, when writers start adding much more, they risk losing their audience.

Bruce Wayne is a straight-laced, determined crimefighter who uses his family's wealth to patrol the streets of Gotham, and for which he wants nothing in return. He has vulnerability issues. The end.

In a different vein, in *The Hunger Games*, Katniss Everdeen has a different, complex passion she brings to that future world where decisions come fast and furious. Where the events of his youth damage Bruce Wayne, they serve to strengthen Katniss Everdeen.

Bruce Wayne has his family fortune to fall back on. Katniss does not.

Bruce Wayne's need to protect his city stems from a childhood without parental involvement. Katniss's willingness to take whatever action is necessary to protect her family stems from her upbringing in a close, supportive family.

Bruce Wayne, as Batman, rarely struggles with the decision between right and wrong because his worldview is stable and unchanging. Katniss sees more shades of gray.

Katniss's story is more intimate than Batman's, too. Whereas Batman is a vigilante with a secret identity, Katniss is a teenage girl who finds herself thrown into waters much deeper than she's had to tread before. Bruce Wayne is a hardened person. He's not going to change much. But Katniss's story is one of youth blossoming into the full authority of her adulthood.

Add it all up, and it says that a writer's challenge in presenting Katniss is a bigger hill to climb than the challenge of presenting Batman.

I know. I know. *(holds up hand)*

I can already hear Batman fans screaming.

Of course, it's important to get Batman right, and of course, that's not an easy task.

But—partially because we see her growing into her prowess (whereas we find Batman when he's already, well, Batman)—Katniss is a more complex character in terms of what her story needs. In addition, the authoritarian land of District 12 in Panem is foreign to us, whereas Batman's Gotham City is a gothed-up version of New York.

Then there's the fact that Bruce Wayne does not change much throughout his Batman sagas. Once the story is done the writer puts him back into his Bruce Wayne box and lets the next person take their hand at him.

Katniss's personality grows deeper through her saga.

So, as a reader, Katniss's saga is going to need more meat to the bone when it comes to depth of characterization.

I need to see where her sense of loyalty and her ability to differentiate right from wrong comes from so that it shines through when she needs to make those split-second decisions that will affect her forever.

Take note, though, this differentiation between Batman and Katniss Everdeen has everything to do with the stories we're telling, the characters themselves, and the situations those stories put the characters in.

ALL RIGHT.

I hear you. What should we be thinking about as we sit down to do this in our manuscripts?

Since readers of Katniss Everdeen need that much more background, how did Suzanne Collins (no relation, by the way) make it work?

Let's look at Katniss from the writer's perspective.

First, Collins chooses to write in the first-person point of view.

This is a standard of Young Adult fiction, which *Hunger Games* most definitely is. It means we are firmly in Katniss's head All The Time. Second, Collins is adroit at picking out the right details for her point of view and bringing them to bear on the story that's coming.

Look at this first paragraph:

WHEN I WAKE UP, *the other side of the bed is cold. My fingers stretch out, seeking Prim's warmth but finding only the rough canvas cover of the mattress. She must have had bad dreams and climbed in with our mother. Of course, she did. This is the day of the reaping.*

WE DON'T HAVE to go any further to know that Suzanne Collins knows her character.

That's step one in this whole adventure, by the way. The key to writing amazing characters that readers will love is for the writer to know those characters deeply and intimately.

But Collins also knows how to write, and she knows that readers need to feel Katniss from page one.

Look at that paragraph.

There is not a wasted word.

I admire that so much in a writer. The confidence in this writing is attractive all by itself.

The first sentence has two meanings. One in the moment, the other conveying the bigger picture of what's happening in the world around her.

Katniss wakes up alone and in a cold world.

There's also the question of who she is reaching out to as she stretches to find warmth only to find it gone. Is it a lover? A friend?

I want to know.

First, though, we learn she's felt only the rough canvas covering the mattress. By this Collins shows us Katniss's world is harsh. Hard. So hard that her sister (we quickly find the answer to that first question) gets bad dreams and has likely gone to the safety of their mother's bed—and since their mother is a loving mother, she takes Prim in. Katniss accepts this, of course. She accepts the hollowness of her loneliness because she loves her sister, and because she understands. Today, you see, is the day when every child is at risk.

It is an amazingly good first paragraph.

Followed by a second, equally perfect paragraph.

By the end of that second paragraph, I understand Katniss's upbringing—and since she tells it in such a simple, loving way, I can't help but already like her.

This is how you do character development in such a compressed space: Know your character. Show us the right details, then get on with it.

Background:
Peeling the Onion
Victor and Klaus Hargreeves

AT THE END of the day, Katniss Everdeen's background isn't *that* complex, but it's important to her story that Suzanne Collins gives the reader a big dose of it quickly.

Compare *Hunger Games,* though, to the Netflix adaptation of *The Umbrella Academy,* and compare the approach to telling Katniss's story to that of Victor Hargreeves.

Unlike *Hunger Games,* where Collins focuses intently on Katniss from the very beginning, the writers of *The Umbrella Academy* don't give me much about Victor early on, at all. Instead, they run a big con game—or perhaps big illusion is a better term for it—that keeps me focused on other areas as they slowly lay the groundwork that will let them reveal Victor's true power and purpose in the multiverse.

At first, I'm led to see *The Umbrella Academy* as Number Five's story because the plot spends an extravagant amount of its time on him, and he is the one forcing the action. And, yes, Five is the primary instigator of the story—especially in the first season.

But everything leads to Victor's big reveal at the end of that season.

And this is even before we get to the transgenderism that the series incorporates while adjusting to Elliot Page's personal transition leading into the third season.

Victor has a convoluted, multilayered background that is so deep and so tortured that, as time reveals each layer, I, the viewer, am asked to reevaluate his situation multiple times.

I absolutely adore that.

While the story structure of *The Umbrella Academy* is different from *This Is Us*, the trick its writers pull off with Victor is similar to the one *This Is Us* manages with Jack Pearson. I see Victor at the end of the first season differently from how I view him at the beginning of it.

The same thing happens in season two.

And again in season three.

How do the writers do that?

"Simple."

They know their character, and they know where they are going.

So rather than mirror Katniss in *Hunger Games*, these writers do some fun things. First, they show us Victor before they show us any of the other Hargreeves siblings. By definition, this is the message that Victor is the main character. They also use a few touches of foreshadowing in the first episode to suggest that Victor's powers—which are said to be nonexistent—are much larger.

Then they push on to use compelling storylines featuring each of the other characters, who are also well-realized, to distract us.

Until that final reveal, though, Victor, Number Seven, is the sad, powerless sibling who never blossomed. The writers show him striving to be an artist, but, due to his own self-restraint, not being able to make it (something that matters in the context of the story). Then Victor finds a compatriot from outside the family who pushes him to unleash himself, and, in the process, we find the full backstory of his character—how poor Victor's polymath father locked him into a soundless chamber as a child.

What I find amazing about *The Umbrella Academy* is that it has not one, but two such powerful characters developed in this fashion.

Victor's brother, Klaus Hargreeves, has a story that is also revealed to the viewers such that his erratic, drug-addicted behavior—which at first seems like simple comic relief—and the slow burn of the writers' reveal of his back story, moves the viewer from seeing him as an entertaining source of that comic relief to a deeply sympathetic persona.

Along the way, we see how his avant-garde sense of absurd humor comes from a place of self-defense against the extreme abuse that he, too, had heaped upon him as a child.

Again, I love this.

Klaus has become one of my favorite characters of all time.

So this is the chef's kiss of storytelling.

The Umbrella Academy uses exposure to the father figure, Reginald Hargreeves, to explore how parents affect the development of their kids.

In this case, Hargreeves is a particularly nasty form of an omnipresent parent, which is, admittedly, fun to watch in story form. Reginald Hargreeves is one of those villains you love to hate.

The Umbrella Academy is a fascinating series to study if you want to see how a writer can present the background needed for character C in the form of primary storylines driven by characters A and B. Its writers reveal these characters' backgrounds in layers that drive home the full extent of the story.

This is a particularly interesting form of misdirection that I always admire.

To interplay storylines that way is great fun and leads to character transitions that I find delightful.

Final Background Checks
Sherlock and Watson

I KNOW writers for whom the only answer to "How much background do you need," is to say "More!" I don't agree, but if we're talking about primary characters I'll not argue too much.

For supporting characters, though, I'm hardline.

The story dictates.

The depth a character needs depends on their part in the story.

Minor characters with limited time on the page won't need deep backgrounds, but the more a contributor interacts with the main characters, the more depth they need. At least so the reader can place them in the proper context.

Consider Sherlock Holmes and Dr. Watson for a moment, a pairing in which Arthur Conan Doyle defined Watson, the supporting character, more fully than he defined Holmes, who is the protagonist. Those stories, however, are about the very mysterious Holmes. Watson is the pragmatic, everyday everyman.

I enjoy these stories specifically because I don't completely understand Holmes. How could I? Holmes is a genius. A savant. He sees things that ordinary humans cannot—and his elite status means he has trouble finding true human companionship for the simple reason that he is impossible to get close to.

I, the reader, am none of the things Holmes is.

Given that, Arthur Conan Doyle cannot let me, as the reader, get too close to him.

It makes sense that he would reverse the polarity for these two.

What I learn of Watson is firsthand.

What I learn of Holmes is legend.

So, it's all fair game.

Upbringing, family, education, work environment, trauma, cultural influences, relationships, significant experiences, and everything else that have shaped who these characters are along the way. How much you need is always a tough call. The tipping point I suggest, though, is always the story.

Give readers too many pieces of background outside of the story, and their eyes will glaze over. Too few and they will find it hard to care.

Let's play with that idea, now, shall we?

Find a few minutes of quiet time, and dwell on one of your favorite characters.

Put them against that framework I just laid out.

What is their role in the stories they populate? Why do they matter? Examine the way their writer presents the character. Note the effort that went into making the character work, and ask yourself why that was enough.

Given the story, why was it important that this character was portrayed as they were portrayed? Especially if that character was given more than a quick brush of background.

Compare them to people in your own life.

Consider the phrase: "They are the kind of person who…"

If you pick any immediately memorable character from any book, movie, or show that you've loved—I'd bet that you could ramble forever on that phrase, so, try it.

While the definition of a personality might always remain more of an *I know it when I see it* than it does any scientific certainty (take that, Myers Briggs!), the truth is that we all *do* know it when we see it. And, in the end, the amount of background you bring to your characters has to fit the story you're telling.

There is no perfect recipe that fits all, so you've got to figure it out yourself. But too much bogs readers down, and too little can make characters dull.

No one said this was going to be easy.

Your goal is to find that Goldilocks zone where everything balances out just right.

Details, Details, Details
Point of View and Voice

A MOMENT of pure shop talk.

While I'm talking about personality, background, and everything else, I should take a moment to address one aspect of the *how-to* part of creating personalities just a bit further.

Most writers understand that a character's personality is defined by an infinitely combined amalgam of interesting traits. And the things I've talked about—and will continue to talk about—in this book represent a massive toolbox by which writers convey these traits.

As writers, though, we get two tools that we don't generally think about when we view characters as everyday people: The first is the ability to control point of view, and the second is voice.

Think about this for a moment.

When we tell stories, we choose the words we use, and we choose what details we allow our characters to give us. Use this wisely, because the goal here is to choose words that the characters would use. This is an important tenet of point of view.

Characters convey their essence through the words they use to describe things. That description gives readers the character's sense of personhood. The example of Suzanne Colline's introduction of Katniss Everdeen works because that entire paragraph is focused on telling us who Katniss is. And that passage comes before we get to anything that defines where that perspective comes from.

When we select a point of view, we're selecting the limits we can use to describe things.

Voice, then, at least when it comes to characters, lies in the way the character strings together thoughts. A Jack Reacher story shall not have long, flowery passages describing forests. On the other hand, *Lord of the Rings* works when Gandalf delves deeply into discussing their choice of paths but will not if Tolkien gives those same passages to Frodo.

The writer's choice of point of view and voice are completely in the author's hands. Focus on how those characters describe things because this aspect of their point of view forms the way a reader will see their personality.

And the details matter.

If I say a cluttered house is a wreck, that says something about me. If I describe that same place as a dump, that says something different.

This gets even more complicated due to the nuances of the differing worldviews of individual readers. Whereas I see a difference between a house that's a wreck and one that's a dump, my wife, while reading through this manuscript, said she does not.

I stand by my view, of course. Just as she gets her own. But it was an illuminating thing to think about when it comes to character creation.

If, as a writer, I have a husband and wife examine the house, and give a factual recital of it as being filled with busted-up furniture and buckling walls to go with a slow leak coming from the plumbing—then have the wife call it a fixer-upper and the husband call it a dump—I'm laying down a framework that helps describe the personality of those two characters.

I DON'T MEAN that a writer needs to give readers paragraphs of flowery prose to create vivid pictures in the reader's mind. Instead, I mean that the writer owes it to the reader to give them the *right* description and that the most important part of that is the description that the characters give to things going on around them.

One perfect word is more powerful than a paragraph of unfocused fluff—even if the unfocused fluff is technically true. Unless that is, the character describing the situation is wildly verbose themselves (and maybe even a bit optimistic and blustery) in nature, in which case, bluster away. It would be fun to put that character in the same carriage with a sourpuss who will rebut our Pollyanna after she uses multiple stanzas of breathlessly excited poetry to describe the warmth of the sun.

"Screw the sun," might be his gruff retort. "It burns my goddamned eyes."

Our sourpuss, you see, is coming off a late-night bender. Or he's angry at the world because he's just learned his inheritance is gone, or … whatever.

Let's say that our blustery optimist is that way because she's on vacation, and she's just come from a perfect massage. She's feeling free now because she's come out of a three-year funk due to a broken relationship, and she's finding the world is open and exciting.

You can see how these two characters might describe the puddle left by this morning's rain differently, right?

Do not waste your character's point of view.

Goals vs. Motivations
Rachel Green and Gordon Gekko

Kurt Vonnegut said that writers need to give their characters something to desire, even if that desire is just a glass of water. That's good advice. But the water gig only goes so far. Eventually, if we want to create truly memorable characters with real meat on their bones, we're going to need to graduate to higher-order goals.

And beyond that, I suggest that the desire itself is not enough. We need to go one step further.

***

Human beings desire things, and those things reveal our inner character. That's so obvious it's easy to gloss over.

But let's hit the brakes and take a moment to notice a piece that's missing from that rule of thumb. That missing piece is the word *why*.

I say that because, while it is true that a person's desires reveal their inner character, those desires are not randomly arrived at. There is another parameter in this equation—and that parameter is *why* the character desires what they desire.

As in: why does our hero want that glass of water? Has he been talking all night long? If so, why has he been talking? Is he at a conference? A dinner party? On a first date?

Has he crash-landed on a deserted island?

If so, how did he get there, and why is there no water?

It's not enough to just give a character a desire. The writer needs to also find a way to let me know why that desire exists and why that matters. The desire has to be useful inside the story we're telling, or the character will be too thin to keep me engaged.

Think about those examples I just gave in which a character wants water. Each one fits a different story. Show me which one I'm reading.

Desires and their accompanying reasons make characters real because desires stem from the combination of a situation and a personality. These combine to make actions and reactions—which then create the story's plot.

Yikes, right?

If I give a reader something to believe in right away, that reader will give me time to make that character real to them—and will even bring their personal framework to my page to make them real in ways that no one else does. Which makes my job both easier and more fun.

How could it be any different, right?

———

FOR THE MOMENT, allow me to get the tiniest bit pedantic.

Throughout my professional life, I've heard people mix the terms *Goals* and *Motivations* as if they are the same things. The business world called them *Objectives* and *Initiatives*, and people were forever fouling them up.

Writers do it, too.

It makes sense to a degree. Most times, in everyday life, it doesn't matter if we mix these things up because we get the ideas, and the difference doesn't matter to the points of our arguments. But when we're thinking about great characters, and more importantly, what it takes to create those great characters, I think it's a real problem.

Goals and motivations are different things.

Let's see if I can untangle them.

IF YOU WANT to see story structure play out, well-written sitcoms are fantastic things to deconstruct. Each episode is a densely compacted short story, and most are not particularly complex. So, in thirty minutes, you can practice finding exactly where the writers hit (or miss) the beats of story structure, over and over and over again.

If you do spend time watching a sitcom, you'll see some beats you think are quite deftly done, and others not so much.

In the context of character study, sitcoms are even more interesting. This is because sitcoms allow writers to build characters in layers. So, a memorable character in a sitcom will often establish itself fully in the viewers' minds over a collection of episodes rather than just one. Once a writer has established the character, that writer is free to mine it in fantastically fun ways.

Long-running sitcoms are then interesting, too, because their success will eventually allow their writers to break the mold of telling stories in single episodes and will instead allow storylines —hence character development—to play out over weeks and even years.

This means sitcoms can be great labs for thinking about character goals and motivations.

In the TV series *Friends*, for example—which you can find these days replaying on an endless loop—episode one introduces the ultra-privileged Rachel Green when she steps into the Central Perk coffee shop wearing a bridal gown. She's a spoiled brat at this point, someone who knows nothing of the world, better yet real friendship. She is superficial and naïve. Very much focused on her little world. But this is also the point at which she decides to fling herself out into that world. For the first time, Rachel Green is going to be on her own.

So, what is Rachel's goal?

When viewed in the context of what the show ended up

being, her long-term goal (which is both unspoken and unknown to her) is to grow up into a responsible adult. Confronted with the aspect of living the mundane life of a dentist's wife, something she always thought she wanted, Rachel feels anxiety. While she may not know what she wants yet, she knows this is not it.

The fact here is that Rachel Green wants to be a full-fledged, self-supporting person, even if she can't articulate that.

In the short term, however, Rachel's needs are more direct. She gets cold feet, and the desire to avoid the trap of a kept life *motivates* her *decision* to leave her fiancé at the altar. After running into Monica, her high school friend, she quickly becomes *motivated* by her need to pay (among other things) rent. Therefore, she sets a *goal* of finding a job.

Note that her goal is deeper than simply acquiring cash. She's also *motivated* by her background and preconceived biases to do something she's interested in—work in fashion. Rachel *decides* to make a *goal* of working in the field. Unfortunately, time pressures and a lack of anything resembling a marketable skillset force her to settle for a low-wage job at the good old Central Perk.

When we look at her set of goals, we see this sets up an interesting dichotomy.

Acquiring her first job is a success because now she can pay her bills (barely), so things get better. But things also get worse for her because—since it's not the job she wants, and because she now sees exactly how limited her résumé is—Rachel sees taking it as a failure. With the benefit of hindsight, viewers can see her taking that first job as the achievement it is. That job moves her down the path toward becoming a fully actualized person. As hard as the going will be at times (I know ... it's *Friends* ... how hard can it be?), she's finally succeeding without her family's money.

Eventually, still *motivated* by a desire to work in the fashion industry, Rachel will find success in achieving her *goal* and work her way into a job at Ralph Lauren. That will be a success for her because she will have earned it.

In that context, we see that the overarching story needs her to initially fail in achieving her bigger goal of working in the fashion industry because she's not yet a real adult. She has never had to work hard to get anything, and her failure is due to her immaturity and her complete lack of being prepared to take on the world as most people know it. Her failure forces her to take that lesser job—meaning that, for Rachel, things get worse. That the situation is fodder for comedy, of course, helps the writers, too!

Comedy is rooted in failure, especially the failure of those in hoity-toity privileged classes.

Only after Rachel has had an uncountable number of try/success and try/fail attempts at smaller sub-goals (which, again, are driven by interim motivations), only then does she succeed in gaining her dream job. Yet, since her true, unspoken goal is to grow up, achieving that job does not mean her story is over. Rachel's story cannot be complete until she's learned how to deal with life's bigger issues. It turns out that the big job is just one, albeit important, rock in the path she needed to take.

As an aside, I consider Rachel Green to be *the* protagonist in the *Friends* series.

She is the character that undergoes real change.

Certainly, Chandler and Monica change, too, but their growth is not as dramatic as the metamorphosis we see Rachel go through. They simply mature.

The others (Ross, Joey, and Phoebe), though older by the end of the series, are not dramatically different people than they were at the beginning.

So, yes, Rachel Green is the protagonist of *Friends*.

This is why its final plot twist hits with such satisfaction. When Rachel says, "She got off the plane," and Ross turns to find her waiting for him, we know her storyline—which took years to play out—is complete.

Anyway, that's my story and I'm sticking to it.

TAKE note of how this motivation/goal relationship works, though.

I am *motivated* to accomplish something that requires money; therefore, I *decided* to set a *goal* of getting a job.

Motivations are external forces. *Goals* are decisions.

Things can get dicey when we talk about motivated people—as in the idea that motivation is an intrinsic quality of that person rather than an outside force.

There *are* those Gordon Gekkos of *Wall Street,* and Mr. Potters from *It's a Wonderful Life,* for whom the checkbook is a scoreboard, and who are truly motivated by money … or are they?

Could it be that the basic desire to win is what motivates Gekko and Potter, and that the money is just a de facto stand-in for that?

This makes sense because the goals people set through their inner motivation can be wildly different for each person.

Bullies want to control things.

Competitors are driven to win.

The desire to become a chess champion requires a certain style of intellectual.

A crafts artisan wants to make the best quilt.

Fun, right?

So, I respectfully suggest that money was not Gordon Gekko's primary driver, but that he was motivated instead by the need to win, which was formed from his family background and may even be augmented by a genetic tendency toward narcissism.

That sounds plausible, now, doesn't it?

Note these last things are external forces, not decisions. In this framework, Gekko's goal is not a specific target for cash (greed is good, and more is better). Gekko's goal is to crush anyone who gets in his way. He wants to win, and he wants to dance in the end zone as he spikes the ball directly into the other guy's face.

In these cases, parsing language again, I prefer to think about the Gordon Gekkos of the world as driven, rather than motivated. What sets them apart is not the goals they set, but instead the relentless dedication they exhibit while chasing their eventual goals.

Stacking Goals
Sarah Connor

Let's look at another highly driven character: Sarah Connor from *The Terminator* movie series.

I unabashedly love her story.

She starts as an everyday party girl and ends as a hardened warrior woman fighting for the future. Like Gekko before her, she is relentless in her work to achieve her goal.

If asked what that goal is, the casual thinker would say "to save the human race." That works for them, but it's a misleading take for writers.

In story speak, Sarah Connor is not trying to save humanity. Not directly, anyway.

I can say that because, in the end, her knowledge that John's survival is important if humanity is to survive is her *motivation*. Her *goal* is to keep her son alive so that *he* can have the goal of saving the world. This differentiation may not matter to a viewer, but it's vital for a writer.

The relentless nature of Sarah Connor's approach stems from the fact that no one believes her. Instead, the world's willful ignorance forces her to employ any means necessary to keep her son alive, which she does.

Her story cannot have her goal specifically be to save the world because this is out of her scope.

When Kyle Reese comes to Sarah's time, the war has not been won or lost. The story James Cameron lays out provides no certainty that humanity will save itself if John Connor survives, but Connor, Sarah's unconceived son, is humanity's best hope.

So, like a relay racer running the first leg, her role is to deliver the baton that is John Connor into the future.

This is a reason why Sarah is so compelling.

She's not yet even pregnant with the future savior, and she has to break down this whole mess.

Her transition is fun to watch.

All that said, it's valuable that viewers see Sarah struggling with the weight of the result if she were to fail. It's important to us that she understands John's goal will be to save the world, and that her actions encapsulate his ability to achieve it.

Because of course it is.

But if we as writers see the truth—that her true burden (hence driver of motivation) is her *knowledge* of what the future holds as compared to the normal world she lives in—then we can present her interactions within that world around her with more force than we could otherwise.

This practice of giving a character a piece of knowledge no one else agrees with is a useful story construct. Watching characters we love bounce against the walls society puts up is frustrating, but we love it anyway. It is fun to see the world around her ignore and impede Sarah Connor despite the importance of her knowledge.

In this setting she transforms (pun intended!) from that meek party girl she is at frame one, into the kick-ass rebel she eventually becomes, not just because she wants to save her son, but because she knows she's right, and because no one believes her.

For Sarah Connor, there is no other way.

If the world had believed her, though, well, the story would have been different, wouldn't it? If the world had believed her, Sarah Connor would have handed off the baton, and then Sarah would have become a Damsel in Distress, and the movie would be nothing but chase scene after chase scene as the Terminator fought its way through the world's defense systems to get at John Connor's prospective mother.

I like Warrior Sarah much better, thank you very much.

Of course, depending on the characters and their stories, these goals and motivations can cascade in messy ways. And sometimes goals and motivations can crisscross in fun ways, too. The writers of Deadpool (who is another deeply complex character) are great at this, for another example.

In real life, we can jumble these goals and motivations together when we're talking like fans because, mostly, we get it. But it's bad logic for a writer of stories to confuse one for the other. Confusing these things leads to stories that flounder around like a shopping cart with a wobbly wheel. They get where they want to go, but don't seem to work out in satisfying ways. Messy stories can leave you with an unhappy experience because, if I get this wrong in my head, the story may not validate properly in the end.

Why does the character want that glass of water, again?

If the character wants that water so they can throw it in their boyfriend's face, that's a different story from one where they want it to water their carrot patch.

At best, if my character's motivations aren't clear, the character (hence the story) may lack believability.

At worst, readers will throw the manuscript across the room and out the window.

If our character's goal is to get a car, then the story's resolution had damned better well include an answer to the question of whether they got that car or not—*and* whether achieving that goal satisfied the itch that created the desire for a car to begin with.

A goal is something a person decides to achieve or accomplish.

Their motivation is what drives them to set that goal.

Reactions
Crash Davis, Meg Ryan, et al

IN THE MOVIE *Bull Durham* (which is flat-out the best baseball movie ever made, and I'll brook no counter discussion), aging journeyman and minor league catcher Crash Davis drops young, hot-headed pitcher Nuke LaLoosh the signal to throw a fastball. One finger. LaLoosh doesn't want to bring the heat. He wants to throw a curveball instead, so he shakes his catcher off with great exaggeration. Davis persists, flashing the same angry finger again.

Again, young LaLoosh disagrees.

This is not the first time LaLoosh has done this in the film. Earlier in the year, LaLoosh wanted to throw heat, and Davis a curve. LaLoosh won that battle, threw the heat, and the batter hit a monstrous home run that caromed off the bull out past the right field fence. The blast was so good it even won the hitter a free steak dinner.

Turns out the kid has not yet learned his lesson.

Two outs in the bottom of the ninth, he's cruising to a shutout, and he's shaking Davis off.

So, what does Crash do?

He stands up and wearily commiserates with the hitter and the umpire—boggling with wry gusto at the audacity of the kid who, after following Crash's lead all game long, is one inning away from completing a two-hit shutout. Exasperated, Crash tells the hitter what LaLoosh is going to throw, then settles back behind the plate. When LaLoosh peers in for the new sign, Crash simply beckons LaLoosh to serve it up.

The hitter proceeds to pulverize the pitch, ruining the shutout.

Davis takes the new ball from the umpire, then stalks out to visit the mound, whereupon LaLoosh, bearing a hound dog sense of disappointment, asks Crash if he gave the hitter a tip. The question is more confirmation than query, though. Davis admits it, thereby administering his lesson quickly and firmly (that no pitcher is so good they can get hitters out on raw talent alone). The next instant, though, Davis gives his pitcher a mixture of sarcasm and snark about how quickly the ball got out of the park, and whether anything that went that far should have a stewardess on it. Then, after a beat of silence between them, Davis simply turns and walks back to home plate.

The lesson is complete.

There's a game to win.

It's a beautiful piece of writing.

And it's all in a deeply understood character reacting in perfectly relevant ways to the situation before him.

I'VE HEARD the occasional writing teacher say that a character's reaction to events *is* the story. I think that's right. Reactions define characters, anyway. At their roots, the steps a character takes in reaction to the world around them are the "Try" part of every cycle.

Reactions—or the lack thereof—also reveal a character's inner moxie.

When a character is well-defined, their reactions to the world around them become memorable because those reactions give readers something tangible to relate to.

In this case, we've all felt like Crash Davis does at this moment.

THIS SET of reactions that Crash has after LaLoosh shakes him off works because the entire string of his reactions (try cycles) aligns with his frame of the world, which then serves so many aspects of the story. That they come one after the other simply adds to the sweetness of the moment.

Let's look at them.

At the time of the events, Crash Davis is an aging veteran. Like it or not, he's not with the Durham Bulls to win games. Instead, his job is to mentor the kid with the million-dollar arm and the ten-cent head.

His day is past, and he knows it. Everyone *else* knows it, too. I think this is an under-discussed part of *Bull Durham.* Everyone around Crash Davis knows that, for him, the dream is over.

All that's left for him is to bleed his knowledge into the kid.

Well, that, and the love of the game.

This scene between Crash Davis and the kid shows us all of that embedded directly into Crash's reactions to LaLoosh and the entirety of the situation around him.

He's annoyed at having to teach this kid a lesson—again—but he takes enjoyment from the kid's stupidity, too. He enjoys the moment by chatting with the umpire and the hitter. That dynamic is a time-honored part of the game he's loved for as long as he's been able to. He understands that his experienced eye and his willingness to lose a battle to win a war will let him pass on to LaLoosh the lesson that talent alone is rarely enough to win.

His reaction is also an acknowledgment of his role.

Crash Davis is a teacher now.

The competition takes a back seat.

He understands his job, and he does it as a good organizational man does. This role is critical to Crash's psyche, too. Crash Davis is an organization man now.

Sure, he's got an independent streak, but Crash has been around long enough by now that he understands he can't change the world. Still, though, he wants to be part of it. For as long as he can have it be, Crash Davis wants to be part of baseball.

Pitch by pitch, out by out, inning by inning, his Crash Davisness lets him enjoy this moment at the highest level possible. Where others might clench up and explode, Crash celebrates the game by talking shop with the batter and umpire.

Live and let live.

Enjoy the moment.

Life is a long game. I hear there's a manager job up in Vidalia.

I enjoy Crash Davis's calculating response to LaLoosh's naïve self-confidence specifically because it shows me the combination of fatigue, frustration, wisdom, and joy for life that I know is flooding through the aging catcher at that moment. His reaction is, pun intended, pitch-perfect, and its execution is relatable.

At that moment, I become Crash Davis.

I understand how Crash Davis loves and respects life (and the game of baseball) for what it is.

Crash Davis is a fantastic character.

As WRITERS, we can mire ourselves in the Try/Fail cycles of plotting and spend hours deciding how Things Will Always Get Worse. And, we *should* pay attention to those constructions. But focusing on that too much can lead to characters who do things they wouldn't normally do, merely because the author needs them to.

We've all read books where the author imposed their will on the characters.

Don't do that.

In the end, reactions are good stuff.

Bold. Direct. Secretive. Evasive.

Reactions are where the interesting things live.

Reactions make our characters come alive.

ONCE YOU'RE LOOKING for them, character reactions are everywhere—particularly when relationships are important, such as in the romance genre, where, while the plots *can* be quite twisted, it is the relationship of the two figures in question that matter.

Things can happen or not, but it's a romance writer's job to ensure they twist the interaction of the two lovers into a tight, unwieldy knot of relationship politics. No interpersonal acrobatics, no romance. Or, in other words, no wild reactions, no relationships.

Watch any good rom-com and you'll find every scene is chockfull of reactions that characters build on top of earlier reactions.

What would *Bridgerton* be without the revolving misdirection and give and take of Daphne Bridgerton and Simon Basset, after all? What is *You've Got Mail*, if not a steady stream of action/reaction events between Meg Ryan and Tom Hanks, each one bringing a smile or a gasp? Or *Sleepless in Seattle*, for that matter—which deftly pulls off this set of interactions without the main characters even being in the same place until the last scene.

Magic.

Romance writers need setting and situation, too, of course. But mostly they need to throw their lovers together in as many intricate and interesting ways as they can concoct. The more unexpected, the better. When that happens, reactions to the events of the story always create new sets of reactions. In that way, I can suggest the romance genre is built on the idea that a character's reaction *is* the next event. In that light, the romance is not so different from the thriller, either—which might feel like an odd set of genres to lay side-by-side, but the comparison works to a degree.

Think about it.

This is because reactions are about emotions, and if the reaction is authentic the emotion is authentic.

Complexity
Elric of Melniboné

IF YOU ARE a longtime fan of fantasy, and the name Elric of Melniboné comes up, you will have an opinion.

Is he a hero? A villain?

Is he powerful or weak?

It all depends, now, doesn't it?

Elric, you see, is a classic antihero.

He has issues.

Here is a quick-blast recap for those readers who are not fantasy fans.

Elric of Melniboné, the primary protagonist in Michael Moorcock's Eternal Champions series, is the last emperor of a fallen and dying people. As such, he is their protector. Their fate is in his hands as he goes through a series of wildly difficult adventures. In the end, Elric is always loyal to his people—or at least as loyal as he can be in Moorcock's odd multiplex of a universe where dimensions shift, and situations rapidly change. Elric's world is one filled with intense magic, much of which Elric needs simply to survive.

He is an "other," too. Albino in appearance. Weak of physicality—at least when not bolstered by that magic, or by Stormbringer, a weapon that acts as his conduit for energy but has a thirst for blood and a mind of its own. Elric's addictions to the magics he needs to lead his people cause him an endless stream of moral dilemmas and choices. His ties to Arioch, a demon god who provides him access to those dark magics, create mind-bending conflicts inside him in which life and death are always at stake—though exactly whose life and death are at risk changes constantly.

At the end of the day, Elric is not a particularly likable protagonist. Except in the ways that he is. And that's part of the mystery of him as a character.

Elric does want the best for people, but he comes with a muddied moral code, and he lives through a set of experiences in Moorcock's adventures that give him so much inner conflict it might melt a normal person. He knows the consequences of his actions, which helps us to suffer with him. And he sees the suffering his actions bring with them, which helps us sympathize with his choices. But Elric is strong enough in his commitment to his goals that he can make the problematic decisions he needs to make, even though his choices are not particularly noble.

In other words, if you're looking for complexity in a character, you've come to the right place.

In a way, Elric is the fantasy version of *Fight Club*'s unnamed narrator (played by Edward Norton). He is Viktor Frankenstein of Mary Shelley's famous book—a man whose very actions can bring him down. These are all complex characters, right? They want to be good people. They want to do the right things. They don't start out intending to do anyone harm.

And yet, things don't quite work out that way.

Complex characters drive amazing stories.

We know complex characters when we see them, of course. But what exactly makes them complex?

For me, it starts with that inner core—that moral center that comes with each character. Once a writer has established that center, they can put their characters into such horrible positions that those moral cores get stretched, bent, and battered, sometimes to the point of breaking, other times to the point where the character doesn't even realize they've been broken.

Think about that.

It's fair to say that we all want what is best for everyone around us but, as they say, the proof is in the pudding, and conflict and stress bring out the true nature of exactly how far our moral codes go.

I'm focusing on the antihero here because I want to make a point about characters that are stretched so far that they do things they didn't think they could ever do.

To be clear, every major character I've discussed in any depth in this book has this element of complexity—a set of core ideals that are relatable and that then get tested by external forces.

That's the point.

Put your characters on the rack and see how they squirm, right? Things get worse. Or, quoting Vonnegut again, be a sadist to your characters.

How the character responds to dilemma, how they choose their paths through the minefields we lay in their path, what compromises they are willing to deal with—that's what exposes a character's complexity. It's what makes them interesting.

I love a good antihero, though, because while the antihero becomes broken, they retain remnants of their otherwise admirable core that are large enough that it still shows through. Antiheroes are good people who—sometimes—do terrible things. When they do, the antihero then pays the emotional price that comes with having done those actions.

If a reader buys the breaking of an antihero, that character becomes iconic.

Think Ender Wiggin in Orson Scott Card's *Ender's Game*, a child prodigy who deals with the ramifications of a horrific war and his part in it. Ender breaks, but he reacts in a way that makes him more of a tragic hero than an antihero. But it's a fine line.

Theo Decker, on the other hand, from Donna Tartt's *The Goldfinch*, is a good person—or at least seems like he could be a good person—but has a deeply flawed and flexible character that we relate to because we see how his inner core breaks after he quite logically steals a painting during a cataclysmic terrorist's bombing that changes everything about his life. Decker is an antihero.

Similarly, Octavia Butler gives Lauren Olamina, from *Parable of the Sower* and *Parable of the Talents,* such a deep, dystopic situation that we can't help but follow and admire her as she creates her own religion, then struggles to reconcile her core beliefs with the harsh realities of her world.

Is she an antihero?

Others can disagree, but I think so.

Olamina is a broken person living in a broken world, but she has a vision, and that vision lets her make harsh decisions—decisions in which some people win and others lose—with a pragmatism that does not always require her to let nuance sneak in. In this way, she is much like Elric of Melniboné.

Let's finish this game with Atticus Finch, Harper Lee's *To Kill a Mockingbird* lawyer, who got an interesting facelift when Aaron Sorkin remade the novel as a play. Lee's Finch is a straightforward hero, though one who loses. Sorkin's Finch moves toward the tragic side but never breaks so far that he becomes an antihero.

It would be interesting to see a revision of his story in which his loss breaks him that far.

This is something that happens when we start thinking about characters, too—or dare I say celebrating them. We push them further in ways we'd love to see them pushed. We think about the *what-ifs* around their stories, and we wonder about what would have happened if they'd just gone left instead of right.

So. Much. Fun.

Each of these characters is complex. But without the writer putting them into tense situations, we would never know about them.

That's the magic.

If we want to build complex characters, we need to take the time to get to know them, then give them serious problems to deal with—specifically, problems that strike at the heart of exactly who they are. We want to love them for their flaws. Suffer with them as they make mistakes but hold them accountable in the way nature holds all such weaknesses accountable.

Focus on their internal conflict as it relates to the world around them.

Show us their struggles, their fears, and their desires and we readers will feel like we know them.

Then leave your characters free to do their thing.

Use of Language
Clone Club

COUNT me as part of the group of people who think that what Tatiana Maslany and her writers accomplished in *Orphan Black* was astounding.

I loved this show.

The writing was amazing.

I embraced the characters, admired the mix of science and society embedded in its existence, and got stuck in the twists and turns of the story.

One actor, a wide range of characters, all of them distinct, each of them fun to watch.

If you've seen the show, you know what I mean.

If you haven't watched the show and want to see a perfect dissertation on the differentiation of character, get thee hence and check it out now.

Sarah Manning, Helena, Cosima Niehaus, Alison Hendrix, and Rachel Duncan are all distinct characters, each believable, each realistic, each with vivid backgrounds, and each—despite being portrayed by the same actor—with their own physicality.

In other words, each character is unique.

Add the side characters of Elizabeth Childs, Katja Obinger, Veena (M.K.) Suominen, and Jennifer Fitzsimmons and you've got a whole baseball team full of amazingly differentiated players. Throw in Krystal Goderitch as the Designated Hitter.

My personal faves at the beginning of the story were Sarah and Cosima, with Alison and Rachel in order behind them. Helena, originally presented as a warped antagonist, was an interesting progression to follow as she went from evil to amazing.

The final turning point for me I think, was seeing her sing "Sugar, Sugar" in the car with Sarah.

Regardless, Helena grew to be another co-favorite—which, I'm sure was among the writers' many goals.

Anyway.

Here's a thing: even though each of these characters is played by the same actor, if I close my eyes and listen as the show plays, I know who is on screen simply from the dialog. And I mean that word, *dialog,* directly. Not the dialect.

In this chapter, I'm going to give you bits and pieces of dialog.

If you've watched the show, you might well begin filling in the accents and dialects of the characters simply because Maslany did such a great job with them that their dialect will pop out. But if you haven't watched the show, you'll still be able to tell the characters apart—or at least see them as separate entities—simply by how they use language. This is because each of the characters has a vocabulary and an approach to linguistics unique to themselves.

Here is the first example of dialog:

"This I like."

It's clearly Helena.

As is: *"Touch her again and I will gut you like a fish."*

Helena has a hard background. Her personality is raw. She has no true education, but is wise and intelligent in the way that comes from living life on the land. She uses words in ways that are close to the bone and completely aligned with her truth. Her language is amazingly delightful at the same time as it is harsh and direct.

Soccer mom Alison Hendrix is a dramatically different person.

Her world is cloistered and safe.

Well, except that an evil corporation is monitoring her as part of a secret program, of course, and that her husband is in on it. But she doesn't know that at first, and what she doesn't know can't hurt her.

Alison has kids. She does school things. She manages the household.

But, of course, she's restless.

There's something more out there for her.

In this light, the line: *"So my bottom line is my children can't know their mother is a freak. Things have to stay on a need-to-know basis,"* is such an Alison line. It wouldn't sound right from Sarah, for example, who also has a child. Sarah doesn't consider herself a freak, for example. And whereas Sarah is militant, Alison simply wants things to be orderly and in control.

In this way, the sentence "Things have to stay on a need-to-know basis," *could* come from any of the four who are not Helena but only Alison would use it in this domestic context.

"She's been poisoned. By Big Cosmetics What about that is confusing?" is pure Krystal.

Obviously.

Breaking these sentences as they are broken might suggest Helena's speech patterns, but from Helena's mouth, the sentence would likely read. "Poisoned. Big Cosmetics. What about is confusing?"

This focus on individual vocabulary is something I struggle with in my writing. I know instinctively that every person has their unique phrasing, and when I'm in the right flow and I can get into the heads of my characters, this comes out well. But the ability to transition into character is a muscle. One I need to keep focusing on lest I get lazy. It can be hard work to get into character quickly, and writing dialog like this requires me to be deeply into the character.

Here are more examples of dialog from *Orphan Black*'s characters starting with Cosima Niehaus, the ultra-brainy biologist who drives much of the Crazy Science vibe that permeates the show.

Cosima is a classic nerd. She's extremely talented in her field, and good enough with the public that she's capable of stepping outside those boundaries, but for only short periods before she gets overwhelmed.

Here's a classic comment from her:

"I'm kind of always late so kind of always sorry."

I'll call this perfect Cosima because the phrase would not come from any other clone.

Sarah would not be sorry to begin with.

Alison would simply expect everyone to forgive her.

Helena wouldn't care what time it was, and Rachel would never be late.

Cosima is also judgmental in ways different from the others. Her phrase: *"No, he's barely a Trekkie. Only went to Comic-Con like once,"* is both great fan service, as well as totally Cosima Niehaus.

Then we come to Sarah Manning, who is technically the protagonist in the sense that we see her first. Sarah is also the clone who stumbles upon the mechanics of the show, and it's her actions that drive the opening acts.

Sarah is a punk.

She's underprivileged. She's got a daughter she can't have control over due to her own general lack of social skills and her awkwardly free spirit that flares up so brightly that she hasn't been able to keep any full-time job. When we meet her, she's just split with her deadbeat drug dealer of a boyfriend.

In other words, despite having an intense sense of loyalty, and a compass that points to true north when it comes to knowing what is right, Sarah is hard to deal with.

She is, at her core, a transactional person. Life is simple that way. Shit on her, she'll shit on you back.

"Shove it up your bleached ass," is Sarah at her finest.

As is *"I'm not giving you shit 'til you give me some answers."*

It is possible, if I squint hard, to hear the first phrase as coming from Alison Hendrix, but even then I think she'd use a full sentence. "You can shove it up your bleached ass" would be more likely.

Small details, right?

But these are the things that make characters pop.

Rachel Duncan, again, also played by Maslany, has a coldness that comes from being raised by a corporation. It is only from Rachel that this line even makes sense: *"We are going to come to terms. The agreement defines mutual disclosure and formalizes contact with what I call Top Side."*

Her self-control and organization sit behind dialog like: *"Even mothers have to do as they're told, sometimes. Don't they?"*

This is full-blooded Rachel.

Its phrasing is so formal it couldn't come from the other mothers. (Alison would use *what* rather than *as*, and Sarah, well, Sarah would tell you to shove it up your bleached ass.)

With the possible exception of Helena, Rachel is the only clone who comes from a hierarchy. Rachel is the only clone who does as she's told.

The entire concept of that dialog means it can only come from Rachel.

Lest you think this *Orphan Black* dialog thing is limited to just Clone Club, here's one for the guys.

It works when Donnie Hendrix—Alison's husband and monitor—says: *"I'm not as perfectly comfortable with manslaughter as you."*

Donnie's personality makes that sentence stick because he's a simple-natured, go-along-to-get-along kind of guy. When we first meet him, Donnie has always just blown on the breeze, so oblivious to what he's doing that he's unabashedly working for the company monitoring his wife.

He will grow over time, which makes him another favorite of mine. But I posit that no other character could voice those words and have them come out as proper. Give Felix (another male character) this line about *his* level of comfort with manslaughter, and you'll deviate from his character. Felix, despite his wild nature, has a golden heart. To speak of manslaughter in such realistic terms would devastate him.

Again, the writers of *Orphan Black* know their characters. They wield their use of language as a tool to differentiate them, and the result is that magic that comes where each is so real the reader can feel them.

IF YOU'RE NOT close with *Orphan Black*, try these on for size: Think how Yoda and Gollum might express the same idea (what a thought, right?). Think about how Luke, Leia, and Han would each voice a command to another character. Consider the difference in the way *The Big Bang Theory*'s Sheldon Cooper phrases a thought differently from Leonard Hofstadter.

Put the same dialog into the mouths of the Joker and Batman and you're risking total discombobulation—even if they are presenting the same thought.

A character's use of language (meaning mostly word choice and use of grammar, but also including timing, sentence structure, and pacing of conversation), not their dialect or accent, reveals your characters' personalities in ways nothing else does. A character's dialogue is formed by education, values, perspective, background, and beliefs. When I'm at my best as a writer, I'm working to ensure my characters speak in ways that are both authentic and consistent with all these things that make their voices unique.

Accent and dialect are valuable, too, of course. When the writer can get it right, anyway.

But there are a limitless number of accents and dialects in the world, and I am just me. It's easy to get something wrong. I mean, sheesh, every individual dialect has its own nuances in tone and pattern. How am I supposed to get them all correct?

The beauty of this aspect of character creation is that while working on getting everything "right," it becomes easier to see how so much of what we might be trying to accomplish with accents and dialect can be carried off in the base aspect of word choice that is inherent in writing good dialog to begin with.

Get the core dialog right, and the character shines through naturally.

Don't believe me?

Here's a final example of a favorite passage between educated science whiz Cosima and the raw, world-smart warrior Helena:

> Cosima Niehaus: *You're very beautiful.*
> Helena: *Thank you. I like your hairs.*
> Cosima: *Oh, thanks. I like your hairs, too.*

It's perfect.

Physicality
James Bond and an Ensemble Cast

YOU WILL STILL OCCASIONALLY HEAR AN OTHERWISE sane-sounding author say you should never describe what a character looks like. These authors say that they want the reader to be able to put themselves into the main character's position—and, they say, if you describe a character, then the difference will bounce the reader out of the story. For my two cents, this is silly. The physical nature of a character is always a big deal.

Bear with me while I walk us through another fun little game.

I'm going to give you a string of names. When I give them to you, I want you to picture them.

Fully.

After each name, close your eyes and draw a mental picture of them. Notice everything the name brings up. Think about that character. Think about their presentation and their personality. Look at their eyes, the shape of their chin. Let their posture settle over you. Think about how they move. Try to remember how they use facial expressions—or don't.

Then open your eyes and go to the next.

Lather, rinse, repeat.

Ready?

Are you sure you're ready?

All right, let's go:

Indiana Jones
James Bond
Lisbeth Salander

Apollo Creed

Jessica Rabbit

The Hulk

Sarah Connor

Jack Reacher

Miles Morales

Spock

I PICKED the list for at least three reasons.

First, since they are all characters in popular movies, chances are good that you, dear reader, have seen them all. Also, they each have very distinct mannerisms. They carry the physical characteristics given to them by the actors who play them (or the artists who drew them) but also go further than the purely physical features of these actors. Think, in particular, about the way each of these characters moves.

Consider their voices.

The lines of their frames. Their genders.

Adding them all up, each of these characters is fully fleshed out with that *in my face* essence that makes them hard to ignore. Say these names and you create pictures in my mind.

Three members of the list—Indiana Jones, Apollo Creed, and Sarah Connor—sprang to life in the movies, meaning they had no book or comic to base ideas on.

Spock was born on television first, then moved to books and movies later.

Jones and Creed have been played by only one actor, so when I think of Indiana Jones, I see a particular incarnation of Harrison Ford (that, interestingly enough, is *not* Han Solo). In that light, Apollo Creed *is* Carl Weathers

And, yes, I know River Phoenix played the young Indy. It's all good. You get what I mean.

The rest, discounting the animated characters of Jessica Rabbit and Miles Morales, have been played by multiple actors across multiple media platforms—which means there is a strong chance that when I say, for example, *James Bond*, you will get a different mental image than I will depending on whether you're a fan of Sean Connery, Roger Moore, Timothy Dalton, Daniel Craig, or any of the others. I find it interesting but not surprising, that if I'm reading a James Bond story, I see *my* version of James Bond— which is, of course, Sean Connery.

Those actors bring different physicality to the roles, though, and that physicality matters.

Sean Connery's Bond is more sophisticated than Roger Moore's, for example. You can see it simply in the way Connery's posture glides over a scene vs. the way Moore's does not.

Daniel Craig's Bond is more battle-worn, and grittier. Again, this is clear even in his movements.

Since you and I may think of different people when we think of James Bond, we, therefore, experience different stories.

Characters in the visual arts have an advantage in that a big part of their physicality comes in a glance. This advantage can also be controversial, though. Fans want what fans want, and the fury of a fan base scorned can turn ugly if a casting decision goes awry.

The difference between Tom Cruise as Jack Reacher and Alan Ritchson is, um, large, but both worked in the character. Kind of. Cruise's smaller stature broke some fans' mental image of Reacher, so his portrayal caused angst.

As our society progresses, similar situations happen relating to the representation of cultures in our characters' backgrounds. Fandoms will get upset when a show or movie signs an actor they don't see as right for the part of their beloved characters.

And, in this case, *right for the part* comes with baggage from outside the storyline itself.

Why is that?

It's because representation, and the identities those cultures consist of, matters.

Physical expectations matter to fans, and that's a double-edged sword when it comes to creating characters that become so beloved that fans attach themselves to them without reservation.

Physicality can be cultural.

It can be based on gender and sexuality.

A character's physicality says things that fans relate to, and when we change that physicality, we risk losing fans.

But this is a book about characters, and primarily about *writing* characters. So let me stop here to posit that the source of most angst here lies in the pen of the author. As a rule, we are the people who start the process. We are the ones who create the templates. Even characters who come straight from the movies start as words on the pages of a screenplay.

Unless writers want to piss off a contingent of fans, they must portray Lisbeth Salander in a certain style—specifically because of how firmly Stieg Larsson portrayed her in his *The Girl with the Dragon Tattoo* series.

Over time, and as the franchise sees more remakes, you'll see casting variances. But if the portrayal or casting of Lisbeth strays too far from expectation, angst from True Fans is certain to follow.

Significant deviation is risky.

Such repositioning can work, of course. With great risks come great rewards. But assuming one could license a reboot, future *Dragon Tattoo* work that positions Salander as a coquettish domestic housewife is going to fight a mountain of friction to gain any traction.

I also enjoy thinking about how the names on that list that were born first on the pages of books compare to those like Jones, Connor, and Creed, who appeared in movies first.

Text-based literature allows readers to imagine a character's physicality before they see it. Until we see a movie, we picture

Lisbeth Salander's deadly composure in whatever way matches our expectations of deadly composure. We see Jack Reacher's size and James Bond's cool-headedness in whatever way we want to see them.

When I was a kid, I read all those Bond books before seeing the films.

The version of Bond in Ian Fleming's books is much more of a close-to-the-vest spy than he is in movies. Which makes sense. Fleming was MI-6 in and around World War II. He was telling spy stories. The gizmos and glamour came along with the films. This means that when I pictured James Bond, I saw someone different from Sean Connery. But, as casting magic has it, Connery's early portrayals were close enough to the source that I never had issues converting my frame of reference. If Roger Moore had been first, I'm not sure my framework would have converted as well—not so much because of how he looked, but because of how he moved and how he spoke. Bond's droll quips coming from Connery feel sharper and more biting than they do coming from Moore, who always gives me a somewhat smarmy sense of humor under his perspective.

Every character you remember is like this.

Everything about their physicality rolls into the way we see them—their temperament, their emotional strength as well as physical strength, their fragility, and their race or gender—everything about them codes into our memory in ways that are impossible to define but are as real as our memories about anyone else.

So, no. I don't subscribe to the line that says a writer should avoid describing their characters. Sure, be careful. Like everything else, there's a balance. But writers of great characters paint whole pictures where none existed previously.

That's the power of character.

Physicality is a big deal.

Do Characters Need to Grow?
The Serial, and the British Gentleperson Detective

THERE WAS a time when characters did not need to grow through their stories. There are also types of stories in which it's fair to say character growth doesn't matter as much as other aspects of the story.

Specifically, I'm thinking about the old-school serial, and how they differ from the modern-day series, and I'm thinking about the detective/mystery field.

When I was quite young, for example, the entire concept of a television series was that the writers took their creations out of the box, gave them thirty minutes or an hour of entertaining stuff to do that came accompanied with a positive moral, and then made sure they could go back into their box for another episode next week. Eddie Haskell was always going to Eddie Haskell. Mr. French was always going to be there to deal with the kids. And Gilligan, the Skipper, the Professor, and Mary Ann were always going to … well … they were always going to do whatever Gilligan, the Skipper, the Professor, and Mary Ann did.

The Idea Story, which is a staple of Golden Age science fiction, has a similar feel at times.

In that kind of story, characters might change, but such change is not necessary. I'm thinking of Tom Godwin's famous short story "Cold Equations," in which a stowaway adds extra mass to a space flight, changing the physics of that space flight in ways that create a moral dilemma—a moral dilemma that has only one answer. The characters in "Cold Equations" certainly learn a lesson, but other than the fact that one of them is going to die, we don't see any great personal change in them. Which, for that story, is fine. Whether the characters change is not the point of "Cold Equations."

Or take Agatha Christie's detective, Hercule Poirot.

Poirot has a long and twisty back story, and he goes through countless events in his thirty-three novels, two plays, and fifty-one short stories (per Wikipedia). But, despite those events, his fundamental character remains intact throughout the whole of his existence. In every story, he is a shrewd intellectual who pits his intellect against the wrongdoers of crimes. It's not necessary to read one story before the other.

Similarly, Christie's Ms. Marple, too, does not change much over the years, nor does a character like Sherlock Holmes—who comes close to having a character change due to his contact with Irene Adler, but really, he just remains the ultra-intelligent polymath to Watson's bumbling everyman throughout the entire series of cases that he cracks.

The Gentleman Detective is an archetype that does not change, and if they do, they don't change much or for long.

Most of the time, though, readers want characters to change.

We want to see the lessons our characters learn mean something important to them, and we want to see them transform into something different as a result because that transformation is often what cements our love and admiration for them.

For readers, that change is an invisible badge of courage.

Who Needs to Grow?
Ender Wiggin, Captain Dan

ORSON SCOTT CARD'S Ender Wiggin, the protagonist of *Ender's Game,* is a notable example from science fiction. He starts as a naïve, but bright, child who is bullied and pushed and molded to the point of serving his people only to find that things are not exactly as he's been told by his elders—those same elders who trained him to battle a ruthless enemy who, it turns out, are no more ruthless than he is, and who may not even have been a true enemy. As the truth of his situation comes to the forefront, that the war he's been fighting is not as virtuous as he believes, Ender changes how he sees the world.

It takes more books before Ender can work fully through this change but, by the end of the story, he's a fundamentally different human being than he was when the story opens.

Ender's Game is a classic because Ender's character arc makes us think about the fundamental nature of humanity through the mechanism of this change.

It's not hard to find growth in the main characters of almost any book or show. Look at them, and you'll see change happen. In even the serials and story types I mentioned before, the characters get at least a bit warped inside the story itself, and sometimes the characters do at least shift slightly over time.

HERE'S A FUN THOUGHT: Writers don't need to relegate the most profound change arcs to main characters only. Sometimes—

when the lead character can't handle the change—we need to pass that role off to a supporting character.

Consider *Forrest Gump*'s Lieutenant Dan. (I'm talking about the movie rather than the book—which are such different beasts that Lieutenant Dan does not even exist in the book.)

Forrest himself cannot change.

He grows older through the film, of course, but throughout his life, Forrest is rock-steady in his representation of the man with a solid heart of gold and a soul wiser than either his years or his intellect would suggest. His goodness never waivers. His soul never fades.

But Lieutenant Dan does change, and that change is profound.

It's fair to make the argument that Lieutenant Dan, played so perfectly by Gary Sinise, is the heart and soul of the story behind *Forrest Gump*.

To put us on the same page, let me summarize.

Lieutenant Dan is Forrest's platoon leader in Vietnam. He comes from a chain of military men and intends to serve bravely. Lieutenant Dan loses both of his legs in a firefight, though. Forrest saves his life.

At that point, Lieutenant Dan loses himself.

Life as he had envisioned it, is over.

Only after suffering a series of harsh events will Lieutenant Dan save himself—with a little of that unwavering support that only Forrest can give.

My opinion here is that Lieutenant Dan's character arc is one of the most compelling of all time. His transformation from a hyper-focused leader of soldiers to a bitter, angry man, to a new, whole person who is at peace with himself and the world, is a testament to the resilience and strength of the human spirit in the face of adversity.

The question, of course, is: how do you, as a writer, make that happen?

Let's take a few pages to look at how the writers of *Forrest Gump* did it with Lieutenant Dan because this storyline is structured with something close to magic.

WHEN WE MEET THE LIEUTENANT, Forrest has just landed in camp. Lieutenant Dan is gung-ho but gung-ho in that snappy, professional way that marks him as a very good military commander with boots on the ground. His first words call Forrest Gump and Bubba Blue *"my* FNGs" (an acronym I will leave for you to decipher). His next words are to dress them down for saluting him because: *"There's goddamned snipers all around this area who'd love to grease an officer."*

Ten seconds on screen, and the writing has already given us who he is.

A moment later, the writers fill in the rest by giving Forrest a few sentences of voice-over to provide Lieutenant Dan's family heritage. We totally buy it. Lieutenant Dan is patriotic, because of course he is, but the foundation of his self-worth is based on his family tradition.

This entire scene takes barely a minute to play out, but it sets the baseline that the writers are going to leverage for the rest of the story.

Watch it.

Then watch the scene, after the firefight, in which Lieutenant Dan later confronts and lambasts Forrest for cheating him of his destiny of dying on the battlefield. *"Now I'm nothing but a freak!"* he grunts at Forrest in the middle of accosting him.

It's another powerful scene, and it ends with the writers giving Lieutenant Dan the words *"Look at me. What am I gonna do now?"*

With those words, the writers show us that Lieutenant Dan's

identity is gone. Without legs, he's going to be bound to a wheel-chair for the rest of his life. He blames Forrest for saving his life and robbing him of his destiny.

Character change is equal parts structure and magic, I think. And that magic comes from someplace inside you. Which can, admittedly, be a bit scary. If you're trying to show a character's change, sometimes you'll need to let yourself be more vulnerable than you're comfortable with.

Think about what it took the writers to put those words into Lieutenant Dan's mouth. *"Now I'm nothing but a freak!"* And *"Look at me. What am I gonna do now?"*

Those are tough words said by someone looking into the depths of his soul and coming out afraid.

The writers have something to say, right?

Which, again, is scary.

It's okay, though. Just breathe.

Let the character do the character's thing. In this case, Lieutenant Dan's *thing* in that scene is to wallow in his despair. In story structure, this point is where his story has finally been set up. Lieutenant Dan is now a fleshed-out character, in a setting, with a serious problem.

The writers aren't done with him, of course.

They are, again, going to let him do his thing.

From there, Forrest and Lieutenant Dan will go their different ways but, eventually, the writers bring them together again. When that happens, Forrest's rose-colored point of view can't see the true situation. But the viewer understands that life's events have now stripped away Lieutenant Dan's purpose. With nothing to live for, Lieutenant Dan has fallen into depression, turning to alcohol, among other things.

This is Lieutenant Dan at his worst.

We see him in his pitiful, fallen state, challenging Forrest about Jesus and taking Forrest into the seedier sides of life. Then, because of what amounts to losing a sarcastic bet, Lieutenant

Dan eventually becomes the first mate on Forrest's shrimping boat.

This sets the stage for the two most compelling scenes in Lieutenant Dan's transformation.

The first is, of course, the storm scene in which Lieutenant Dan climbs the mast during Hurricane Carmen and has his moment in which he challenges God to a battle. *"Come and get me!"* he screams as the hurricane pours over him. Later, after he survives, he finally thanks Forrest for saving his life, then dives into the ocean for a swim.

The second is his last scene, his validation scene, as it were, where we find him standing again. He's cleaned up, wearing a suit, with a fiancée on his arm, and walking on a set of prosthetic legs made of titanium alloy. *"It's what they use on the space shuttle,"* Lieutenant Dan tells Forrest.

They don't share many words after that, but Lieutenant Dan introduces his fiancée to Forrest, and we know that Lieutenant Dan is planning for a long future ahead of him. We also know that without Forrest, this future wouldn't have happened. When Forrest introduces Jenny, his own soon-to-be wife, Jenny tells Lieutenant Dan *"It's nice to meet you, finally,"* and kisses him on the cheek.

Put those words into the context of Lieutenant Dan's story as a Vietnam veteran.

"It's nice to meet you, finally."

Then that kiss, that soft and gentle kiss accompanied by Jenny's hand placed warmly on Lieutenant Dan's cheek, that tiny detail of a kiss that welcomes him home.

Finally.

Just thinking about that moment can get me choked up.

Notice the writing in each of these moments.

In each case, Lieutenant Dan addresses Forrest, but he's really addressing the viewer, giving us exactly what they need to hear and trusting that we'll be able to interpret it for ourselves.

His writers let Lieutenant Dan talk, and in doing so, they allow him to tell the reader in simple statements how he feels about what's happened and what he plans to do next.

That alone is enough.

That's what Lieutenant Dan does, anyway. And if it's good enough for him, well, it's good enough for your character, too.

Power Dynamics
Lt. Daniel Kaffee, Lt. Cdr. JoAnne Galloway, Lt. Sam Weinberg

Until the last chapter, everything we've discussed so far has been about the individual character.

Their personality and personal makeup. Where they come from. How they use language, and the kinds of things they are attempting to accomplish.

The chapter on reactions broke that frame to an extent because therein I suggested that a character's reactions to the world around them also make them who they are—which directly brings in the external world. I said that, when done well, a character's reactions to external situations are what makes them so memorable. I will always remember Colonel Sherman Potter, an ex-cavalry man from *M*A*S H* shooting a jeep that Major Frank Burns had squashed with a tank.

That's what a cavalry man does, after all. Shoots his disabled horse to put it out of its misery.

Let's take this a step further, though.

Let's talk about power dynamics between characters, and how exploring the way they deal with those dynamics can help us draw out the purposes of the stories we are telling. Power dynamics are important because we know how power dynamics influence us in real life. We behave differently when the boss is in the room than we do when the boss is away. We have a different lingo with our friends and equals, but that dries up when a person we see as an All-Star enters the conversation.

Characters often need to have meaningful relationships with

others of different social strata, who, of course, are all trying to live their own lives within those same social structures.

Sometimes those social structures completely define the stories embedded in them. *Downton Abbey*, anyone?

Understanding and presenting these power structures well goes a long way toward creating interesting and full characters. Positive, negative, or anything in between, these relationships should be an important part of the character's life. They shape who the characters become.

I'm going to focus on the military, though, because those structures are universally understood.

The power gap that exists between military ranks frames my example with Colonel Potter and Major Burns. Burns reports to Potter. That changes things.

In that light, let's talk about *A Few Good Men*, a play by Aaron Sorkin that was later adapted into a quite famous film (famous especially in my little family, where we watched it … well … often).

The entire story is about power dynamics and the order of priorities those dynamics drive.

The three main lawyers in the story are Lt. Daniel Kaffee (Tom Cruise in the movie), Lt. Cdr. JoAnne Galloway (Demi Moore), and Lt. Sam Weinberg (Kevin Pollak). They are all Navy. They are going to be investigating Marines. Which, if you think wouldn't matter, would make you massively wrong.

Kaffee is the lead defense attorney. As brilliant as he is, he gives a disinterested vibe when it comes to his work. He's a guy who gets by on that sheer brilliance alone.

Daniel Kaffee is going places simply because of course he is.

Sure, Kaffee is in the military, but this is a passing thing. For Kaffee, the entire Navy gig is something he's simply going to endure (and even play with) until his stint is over and he can get on with creating his private practice. When he's assigned the case of two Marines accused of killing another, he thinks for a half-second and spits out the plea deal he'll be able to arrange.

This is the world for Kaffee, you see. In and out. Make it happen. I've got softball practice in a half-hour.

Watching Kaffee work, I get the idea that he understands military rank with the distance of someone who deals with the system every day, but in the end does not find it particularly important because he doesn't intend to be around for long anyway. Rank's value is that it gives him an idea of who he needs to talk to and how he might be able to make different deals.

Galloway is Kaffee's opposite in every way. Female, organized, dedicated, competent, and getting by on work ethic over raw brilliance. Not that she's anybody's dummy. Jo Galloway is a smart woman. But she does not have that dazzling, lightning bolt brilliance that rolls off Kaffee every time he so much as crunches an apple as he's describing his background. She out-ranks Kaffee, and she's unhappy that her command structure assigned him to the case because she wanted to be the defending council.

Of course, they are going to clash.

She thinks the clients are innocent, and she does not intend to settle.

Then there's Weinberg, who has no responsibilities here whatsoever. Or at least that's how he describes himself during their first get-together as a trio. Weinberg is the grunt of the litter. He's going to do the real research, though. He's competent and steady. He's responsible. The quintessential good, invisible, workaday lawyer who is going to gouge out a good living over a long life. Weinberg is assigned to the case because even the higher-ups know they can't leave Kaffee unsupervised. While Weinberg can't boss Kaffee around, his personality and his sense of all that is good is strong enough that Kaffee can use it as a rudder when things get tough.

In this way, Weinberg is to Kaffee as Watson is to Holmes.

Early on Galloway uses her command position to force Kaffee

to do things he doesn't want to do. He rails against her, but he's in the Navy now, and when push comes to shove, there is no denying a superior officer's command. She pushes him to dig deeper, a process that includes an awkward trip to Guantanamo Bay (and a complex lunch with the well-established Colonel Nathan Jessop played by Jack Nicholson in the movie).

Without the power dynamic between Kaffee and Galloway, there would be no trip.

Without the trip, there would be no story.

But it's these power dynamics that wind up shaping the characters' growth, too. Kaffee and Galloway, especially. The control Galloway has over Kaffee gives him time to see how firm her resolve is. When she forces him to confront the truth underlying the case, her persistence also forces him to decide what his true feelings are about justice. This is because he sees where Galloway's resolve comes from, and he knows she's right.

As writers, think about this story progression.

In the first act, Kaffee follows her because she presses the issue, and he has no choice but to take the directions of a superior officer. That's what the military does, after all. Even Kaffee knows better than to ignore this.

The last reel sees him using her inner core as a guiding light.

In between, we watch as he teams up with her, not due to her command position, but instead because he wants to be a good person as well as a good lawyer, and she's showing him what that means.

At the same time, as Galloway works with Kaffee, she sees that under his cavalier attitude, he does love and respect the law. He has a bit of a secret, though. A problem dealing with his family background—something she and Weinberg both help him come to grips with.

Weinberg acts as the glue that holds it all together, helping the over-aggressive Galloway give Kaffee the space he needs when he needs it, and helping Kaffee confront his inner demon.

The power relationship Weinberg has with Kaffee, in particular (equal in rank, stronger in emotional balance, but inferior in raw talent), is a necessity to allow him to have the access he needs to affect Kaffee as he does.

As the case unfolds, the power dynamics between them dissolve and the three become a true team, each focusing on their strengths—each with roles and purposes, and each vital to the effort's success.

It's brilliant and totally works.

OF COURSE, *A Few Good Men* does not stop there when it comes to power dynamics.

Sorkin sets it in the world of the Navy and the Marines, which, under the calm surface of the services, have a confrontational relationship that is perfectly voiced by Lt. Jonathan Kendrick—a Marine on Guantanamo who says he likes Navy boys because when the Marines need to hit a beach, the Navy is always there to give them a ride. Sorkin shows us a parallel power structure to the one between Galloway, Kaffee, and Weinberg as we follow Jessop, Kendrick, and Jessup's second-in-command—Lieutenant Colonel Matthew Markinson—as they work to thwart Kaffee's inquiry.

I CHOSE *A Few Good Men* for this topic because these power dynamics are so easy to see, and because they are so obviously critical to the story.

But power dynamics like this exist in every work.

Look for them.

Think about this as you look at your current story.

What power dynamics are in play?

Why do they matter?

What are they going to say in the end, and what do you need each of these characters to say or do to make part of that point?

Pick a book. Any book.

Read a passage between two or more characters and determine what kinds of power each character has over the other, and by what methods those powers have come to exist.

It might be going too far to say that every single conversation made between every single character in every single story has a power dynamic going on. But it might *not* be going too far, either.

Sometimes the power structures may not be as obvious as they are in the military (or in a corporate environment), but even interactions between friends have power struggles going on (see: *Mean Girls*). Every environment has them.

The next time you react strongly to interactions on the page, ask yourself what the power dynamic is between those characters and how that dynamic affects each character's response.

The next time you're stuck in a place, ask yourself which character has the power position and what that position means to them.

If you haven't thought about power dynamics between your characters, I think you'll be surprised at the answers.

Supporting Characters
The Mary Tyler Moore
Show, Westworld

IF YOU ARE LIKE ME, there is a very real chance that some of
your favorite characters are secondary, or supporting, characters
(like Lieutenant Dan). At least that's what Hollywood's Academy
Awards label them. They are played by "supporting actors" and
"supporting actresses," anyway.

Since they are "supporting," it becomes easy to think of them
as less important. This is a mistake, though. These supporting
characters are critical.

Supporting characters help create the basic plot of the story.
They act as relief valves for authors at certain key points of a
story—often being able to explore territory that the main characters cannot. Hence, they allow us to delve into things we
wouldn't otherwise be able to get into without compromising the
main character.

Supporting characters are special things. Unique unto
themselves.

While protagonists speak of the human condition, supporting
characters speak of the world around that condition. Technically, I
say this makes them unique parts of the story's setting.

That's the basis I use to suggest that you can go a long way
toward thinking of supporting characters as if they are the people
version of worldbuilding. If that idea—that supporting characters
are tools writers use to create their setting, and specifically to
build worlds—strikes you askew a bit, all I can do is ask that you
keep it in mind as I go on in this chapter. Because I'm going to
delve into (dare I say celebrate!) several examples of supporting

characters who I find fun or delightful or … well … interesting and memorable for a variety of reasons.

As I brush over each, ask yourself how that character defined the world for its main characters.

Think about that again the next time you're reading a terrific book or watching an engrossing film. Every character moves the plot or at least adjusts it a touch. But whereas the main character carries the burden of the story's thematic device, these supporting characters go a long way toward comprising the *world* that confronts or comforts our main characters.

This is also a reason you might remember a supporting character before you remember the main protagonist.

When I think of television's *Will and Grace*, for example, there's a good chance I'm going to envision Jack or Karen before I get to either Will or Grace. And if I do hit on Will or Grace first, it's almost certain that I'll toggle to Jack or Karen within moments. This is because, being on the page for less time than our main characters, we can afford our supporting characters to get up into the reader's face more often. If we don't go too far, we can let them edge toward being overly bold and over-the-top. And overly bold, over-the-top characters are memorable characters.

Going back to our little game, how do *Will and Grace*'s writers use Karen and Jack to build the world? How do Karen and Jack frame reality for their viewers?

It's fair to say that writers often don't go as far as we could with supporting characters because we don't think of them as important set pieces. We don't spend enough time in their heads, and don't let them go to the extremes we might find useful. Therefore, we leave story on the table.

ASIDE — MY USE OF "EXTREMES" here is meant to include characters of every type (gender, personality, physicality … introvert and extrovert … whatever) who are far over the edge of that type. Support characters need not be extravagantly gregarious or flamboyant to be both useful and memorable, but it helps if they are intense in the focus of their base character. Don't believe me? How many Winnie the Pooh fans don't remember Eeyore? Who doesn't remember Pig Pen?

FOR THE OLD farts among us, *The Mary Tyler Moore Show* is the best example of a long-running, world-building exercise that its writers built on the shoulders of otherwise supporting characters.

It features the incomparable Mary Tyler Moore as Mary Richards. But as good as her lead character was, I think the reason it ran for so long was the amazing collection of Lou Grant, Rhoda Morgenstern, Murray Slaughter, Ted Knight, Sue Ann Nivens, Georgette Franklin, and Phyllis Lindstrom—several of whom were so strong on their own that the network spun off other stand-alone series based on them.

Examining them closely, we see that each represents a different type of extreme personality that the writers use to create —or resolve—issues for the main character. Every one of these supporting characters is interesting on their own merits, but each also connects to Mary in ways that stretch her and enrich her situation for better or worse.

A more modern example: *The Matrix* trilogy gives us the wise and battle-hardened Morpheus and Trinity to offset Neo's naïveté.

Another more recent example would be the recent HBO *Westworld* series pitting two main characters against each other in Dolores and The Man in Black (I'll leave it to you to decide which is the protagonist and which is the villain). The entire storyline is bursting with robust supporting characters that include Bernard, Teddy, Maeve, Charlotte, and the original mastermind of it all, Dr. Ford. (Aside, I love the idea that Ford and Bernard—the instigators of the whole storyline—are such major influences as supporting characters. I did a similar thing in my fantasy series *Saga of the God-Touched Mage*. It's great fun.)

If you're a fan of *Westworld,* have some fun and mix and match those characters. Why do they work together? What, for example, separates Dolores and Maeve? How do Teddy and William line up against each other? Or Bernard and Ford?

Then mix and match.

Dolores, as the lead robot, is an extremely interesting comparison to Ford, who was her programmer. She has his vision. And she has his drive. But unlike Dolores, Ford seems to think he's going to win, regardless, and that winds up being his downfall. In this way, Ford becomes a tragic hero, a modern-day Viktor Frankenstein.

As a writer, I look at how the writers used their arc, and I simply tip my cap.

Teddy, Dolores's cowboy love interest for another example, is perfectly formed to let the writers show us Dolores's drive. I enjoyed watching Teddy grow on his own. Then I had my heart gutted at his eventual fate.

It's fun, isn't it?

Regardless, look at every one of these support characters and ask yourself how they serve to build the world for the protagonists.

Westworld's extreme bending of timelines was a difficult haul, though, so if *Westworld* wasn't your cuppa, do the same exercise with your favorite book or show. Write down the list of characters you remember, their traits, and overall goals, then link each pair and contrast them while asking yourself those same questions about how they serve the protagonist.

Then look at your work, and do the same.

Are there problems?

If so, what can you do to make these supporting characters serve the story better?

See what I mean about supporting characters adding depth and complexity to the main characters?

Do this with your own favorite stories.

It's great for the learning you can get, and fun because it's an outstanding excuse to revisit the warm, fuzzy feelings those characters give you.

A FINAL EXAMPLE: For my money, the first Indiana Jones movie is made what it is by the inclusion of Marion (played by Karen Allen), who exposes the seedier side of Indiana's personality, which then plays into the idea that he's a deeply driven man, even foregoing human relationships in pursuit of his archaeological goals.

So, yes, great fun.

My science fiction series *Stealing the Sun* comes with a full cast of characters, several of whom drive the show at times. While Torrance Black is the main protagonist through the primary storyline, I made it a point to ensure that the end of the series gives each their own resolution and validation. In that way, I was telling more than one story, but I could use each character's arc as foils for the others—advancing the overall plotline by letting the supporting characters play important roles, and at times having them get in the way of each other (on multiple planets, even!).

Making this happen requires the writer to know their characters fully. It helps if you find them fun, or if there's a way you can get into their shoes and live vicariously through them—which, in the case of characters who are not you, or who require you to explore your more vulnerable self, can be more than a little scary. But that's also part of the fun.

Over time, as a writer gets familiar with being more exposed than they might like, this comes easier.

This is a muscle we need to build, and we can only build it by exercising it often. Focus on your characters. Let them be who they are and accept them for that.

Then go even further.

That's a major ingredient in the magic sauce when it comes to making great supporting characters, just like it is for protagonists. It's fair to say that—since supporting characters can be bolder—becoming those supporting characters can teach me more about who I am than becoming my protagonists can.

As in all things, one can go overboard.

The balancing act of providing screen time to supporting characters while working to keep the story's plot moving forward is just that—a balancing act that depends on factors that include story length, genre, pacing, and the complexity of the plot.

Bottom line: writers should tailor the depth of their supporting characters for the story they are telling. Don't short-sheet them, though. A writer can cover a wide span in a little space.

A story like the long con in *The Sting,* for example, required an extensive list of characters, but only a handful needed more than a brief introduction. The movie felt deep, though.

It took almost no screen time at all for *Star Wars* to show us that Lando Calrissian was a smooth-talking scoundrel of a space pilot. Same thing with *Game of Thrones* and Brienne of Tarth, who we understood was a woman of substance and quality from the moment she arrived.

To come full circle on our latest game, take a moment to scan each of these characters again.

How do they define the worlds they live in?

How do they help bring out the nature of our protagonist?

Why does that matter?

What would the story be like if the writer had left that character out?

And, finally, to drive home my little argument: How is that different from world-building?

When given their due, supporting characters can be just as memorable and important as the main characters.

Invisible Characters
Luther

THERE IS another level of character—beyond the protagonist and the supporting cast.

It's the bit player. The extra. The background character sits around and does nothing more than make the world feel right. I'm calling them invisible characters because we're not supposed to see them, but without them, the world goes dark.

And, no, by invisible characters, I'm most definitely not talking about the classic *Star Trek* redshirts, though I promise there will be more on them later.

There is magic to making these characters, though. To not spend time casting that magic is to risk making the reader unhappy.

No one wants an unhappy reader.

AS A LOOK UNDER THE HOOD, I originally titled this chapter with the heart-warming phrase *Tertiary Characters*. I wasn't sure how to classify them, and I figured we sometimes call supporting characters *secondary,* so why not use the phrase tertiary?

I mean, other than the fact that I hate it?

But, as fate would have it, I was driving down the road with Dean Wesley Smith, and he used the phrase *forgettable characters.* I liked that better, but later I realized that I had stored the phrase in my memory as *invisible characters,* which I now like even so much better than Dean's.

So, there we have it. A peek inside the process.

Invisible characters are the people—or other sentient creatures—we use to make things happen but who are not germane to the point of the story itself (though it helps if they draw focus in the right directions). These characters help writers flesh out their worlds. They help us present a place or a situation that's true, deep, and meaningful, but then they kindly disappear and let us go on our way.

If our story happens at lunchtime in New York, after all, we need the reader to feel the rush of foot traffic. If the story happens in a diner, we'd better have the cook or server in the right place and brushed with the correct strokes. If the diner is, instead, an upscale restaurant in a space station around Io, we'd best have the clientele and service processes reflect that.

If you buy my theory that supporting characters are a major element of world-building, then these extras are additional forms of the setting. Not as directly important as the supporting cast, but still important to get right.

So, by *invisible* I most definitely do not mean unimportant.

Invisible characters *are* important, but if done well even the most important of invisible characters will not be a focus of fan conversation.

Sometimes these invisible characters—the bit players rather than the background extras—do go on to interact with the protagonist or supporting characters. They might even have a line or two. Or sometimes they just make an appearance and cast an important, desperate glance.

The portrayal of Katniss Everdeen's sister and family, for example, is critical to *The Hunger Games*. They have active roles in the opening scenes, but once they do their parts, the story moves on. Everything about them forms the basis for Katniss's future storyline—but beyond providing motivation and situation, they no longer drive the story in any tangible way. It would be hard to call them supporting players, but without them, the story would miss something, and hence feel too slight.

Think about that: If you read a story and like the characters, but still feel like things are missing, there's a better than even chance that the setting is broken. In that case, if the writer has given us all the tactile and sensory elements we've come to expect from our stories, I'd suggest casting an accusing gaze toward the world's invisible characters. Odds are good that they have not been fleshed out to the level you need, meaning the writer hasn't done enough work on these invisible, but important characters. They are too cardboard. Too cliché, or too stock.

When a good writer uses these characters well, some incredible things can happen.

For example, take Luther, the newsstand operator in *A Few Good Men*. Even if you've seen the film, I suspect you rarely, if ever, think of him. But by simply saying his name right now, I'd also bet that he flew into your head fully formed. He is a perfect invisible character. He disappears into the story (Luther has almost nothing to do with the plot itself) but is so well-written and well-played that if you work at it, you can bring him back up. He's entertaining, and he provides a road-weary sense of levity at a few key moments.

He also gets a name, which is unusual for a bit-player like that. It is a good rule of thumb to err on the side of not giving these invisible characters names, and if you do name them, go with something bland. Names like John, Ann, Beth, and Bill work in the US culture.

But Luther, beyond simply getting a name, gets an interesting one.

Why is that?

Why does Luther get a name and, say, the server who brings Kevin Bacon and Tom Cruise their beer does not?

The answer, in my mind, lies in Tom Cruise's character, Daniel Kaffee. Kaffee, you see, is gregarious. Also, despite his indifference to his job when we meet him, it turns out that he's also going to be a good leader once he grows up and accepts his place in life. Aaron Sorkin could have gotten by and given us a stock news store operator, and the story he was telling would still work. But, instead, he uses Luther as something more than a simple pressure valve in the story. He uses Luther to show us something about Daniel Kaffee that Kaffee himself doesn't even really know yet. Luther is extremely deep for a bit player because Sorkin uses him to show us that Daniel Kaffee does care about people.

Which is amazing.

Say what you want about Aaron Sorkin, but the man knows his character.

IF THE OPPOSITE HAPPENS, and you're faced with a wall of characters who really should be invisible, but instead are so dense you can't keep them all separate, you've got the opposite problem. Your invisible characters are taking up too much space. You're signaling to the reader that they need to pay attention to them, which bogs down the story.

Aside – I listened to a podcast recently in which the writers were discussing a book in which chapter one introduced twenty-eight named characters. Yikes! I hate to suggest that rules of thumb are universal, and I've been accused of using too many named characters myself, but I question whether anyone can pull off twenty-eight named characters in chapter one.

Navigate those waters at your own risk.

So, yes. These invisible characters are inherently part of your story's setting. Get them wrong, in either direction, and the story won't work as well.

It will serve us well to spend a little time focused on these characters.

So, tonight, or tomorrow, or whenever you're next settling in to read your favorite new book or watch your favorite show, I suggest you do just that: watch for invisible characters. Note how writers use them. Decide for yourself how they entertain and help to move the plot forward, even if, in the end, these characters don't really matter.

What do their physical presence and appearance add to the decor of the scene? What does it say about the story?

Do they get a name? If so, what is that name, and how is it used?

Then do it again for another book.

And another.

Watch how one writer does things that others don't.

Like all the exercises, it's an interesting process.

If you haven't done it before, I promise you'll come away with a greater respect for how your favorite authors think about and use characters.

Sidekicks
Trapper John, B.J. Hunnicutt, and a Cast of Many

IN THE SECTION on supporting characters, I chose to point at *The Mary Tyler Moore Show* as an outstanding example of a broad cast of supporting characters. I debated, however, using the example of *M*A*S*H*, instead. I decided not to, though, because, in Hawkeye Pierce and the combination of Trapper John McIntyre and B.J. Hunnicutt, *M*A*S*H* has something beyond supporting characters. Instead, in Hawkeye Pierce and the pair of Trapper John and B.J. Hunnicutt, *M*A*S*H* has a classic hero/sidekick combination to ride on top of that wide pool of supporting characters (Frank Burns, Margaret 'Hot Lips' Hoolihan, Radar, Klinger, Colonels Blake and Potter, Father Mulcahy, and Major Charles Emerson Winchester III, chief among them).

Mary Richards does not have a Trapper John or a B.J. Hunnicutt in her life, and if she did then I think that would break the whole idea of her character. Her lack of such a strong sidekick is inherent in the underlying aspect of the show's conceit: that Mary Richards is making her way through the world on her own.

A true sidekick would get in the way of her story.

Hawkeye, though, is another thing completely.

Hawkeye needs a wingman—if nothing else simply as a cohort to help him make it through the Korean War with what little of his sanity might remain.

A sidekick is a supporting character, but one with a unique flavor.

Sidekicks are usually close friends—or at least have a closer relationship with the main character than others do. They are assistants, subordinates, or protégés.

Whatever that relationship, sidekicks are on our hero's side.

They help the protagonist out. They conspire. They tell jokes with the hero—or can use the hero as the butt of jokes that other kinds of characters can't get away with. Though often not front and center, a sidekick is a confidant. They have insight into things in the hero's life that sometimes not even the hero sees. A sidekick enriches a story by adding depth to the main character that otherwise would be harder to pull out.

Sidekicks are loyal and dependable, even if they sometimes don't want to be. They are willing to go beyond the norm to help the pair succeed. And sidekicks bring a distinct set of skills to bear on the problem at hand.

Of equal importance, a sidekick also brings a different personality into the story—something that can then go a long way toward making them memorable.

In *Saga of the God-touched Mage*, I gave my protagonist (Garrick) a reluctant sidekick (Darien) specifically because I needed someone to be a sounding board for the reader. Garrick faces weird goings-on in his life (dealing with sects of sorcerers and godlike entities will do that to a person). By adding Darien into the mix, I had someone who could digest and interpret things from a more practical position, and who could either ask questions or point certain facts out that Garrick needed asked or pointed out.

Without Darien around, I would have needed Garrick to perform mental acrobatics that would have made him less believable.

Beyond driving a storyline, Darien bridges the gap between the protagonist and the reader. He also allows me to shield Garrick's behavior from the reader at times.

Think about how Sherlock Holmes's loyal sidekick, Dr.

Watson, is employed at times to divert attention from the mercurial detective while Holmes performs his tricksy magic.

Cool, right?

I think that's important for a writer to think about when developing a leader/sidekick relationship. The sidekick needs to fill holes that the lead character can't cover—or, put in a different frame, a lead character needs a sidekick when they have issues that the writer can't convey easily without one. Even if Arthur Conan Doyle could have given us a direct link to Holmes while making his detective stories work, Holmes does not seem like he'd be a particularly fun character for a reader to have directly in their heads all the time. Watson, the sidekick, is much more relatable.

So, you ask, just who are these sidekicks?

A sidekick can be a protégé—like Robin is to Batman. Robin is skilled in his own right, and he helps Batman fight crime in Gotham, but there is never any doubt about who the top dog is.

Della Street is Perry Mason's business subordinate, but also serves as a sidekick, especially in the recent reboot.

A sidekick can be a sibling, a spouse or a lover, or something ambiguous, as in the case of Xena the Warrior Princess and her sidekick Gabrielle, who have a controversial romantic element to their relationship that is mostly off the page.

A sidekick can even be a random stranger thrown into the fray by happenstance.

Lois Lane is a significant other who serves as a sidekick.

The hijinks that arise as part of her lovers' triangle with Superman and Clark Kent helped to expose Superman's personality. Interestingly, in Jimmy Olsen, the Kent/Superman writers give him a second sidekick role, which makes some sense here, too. Jimmy Olsen serves mostly as Clark Kent's sidekick, whereas Lois Lane supports Superman. Two identities, two sidekicks.

When you start thinking about sidekicks, all sorts of things start rolling in.

Hobbes is Calvin's stuffed tiger in Real Life but is a perfect sidekick in the world that matters. Just for fun, compare Hobbes to Winnie the Pooh's Piglet. Snoopy is a loyal sidekick to Charlie Brown, but Snoopy has that cool style that Good Ole Charlie Brown could only dream about.

It's fun to think about these things, isn't it?

Sidekicks are everywhere.

They are special relationships that serve to spice up a story.

Buddies
Thelma and Louise,
Butch and Sundance

I LOVE A GOOD BUDDY STORY.

Two minds are better than one, right?

It's fun to see two people getting along and essentially collaborating on solving problems.

The line between a buddy story and a sidekick story is sometimes a fine one, but I think it's helpful to think about and know the difference. Batman and Robin, for example, are a mentor and sidekick. Thelma and Louise are buddies. Donkey is Shrek's sidekick. Butch Cassidy and the Sundance Kid are buddies.

The difference is the sense of authority each of the characters has in the story itself.

There is a reason the examples I used above come from properties titled as they are:

Batman

Thelma and Louise

Shrek

Butch Cassidy and the Sundance Kid

BATMAN AND SHREK are the title characters, Robin and Donkey are sidekicks.

Thelma and Louise, and Butch and Sundance are equal partners.

Buddy relationships are fun because neither character holds a stronger position in the story than the other. Since the two are different people with different strengths, one might lead a portion of the story, but in the story's construction, neither is in control. Neither is subordinate. The pair fails or succeeds together.

In this way, the best buddy pairs are like binary stars, constantly orbiting, and constantly swapping positions. Consider *Lord of the Rings*. Gimli the dwarf and Legolas the elf. These two would never come together under normal circumstances. But over the run of the story, they become heartfelt friends and an iconic set of buddies as they work together to achieve shared goals.

Will and Grace is a buddy story, too, because, while both are fully capable people in their professional fields are both equally lost in their personal lives, neither is above the other in the context of the world around them. This is made even more obvious by the fact that Will is gay, hence removing even the traditional power dynamic of male over female.

Not surprisingly, the title carried both names.

Going back to my examples where different sets of main characters are set against strong supporting casts, we see that writers can have fun embedding the buddy construct inside ensemble casts, too.

Mary Richards of *The Mary Tyler Moore Show* was a lone wolf hero in an ensemble cast of supporting characters.

In *M*A*S*H*, Trapper John and B.J. Hunnicutt were sidekicks to Hawkeye Pierce, but they were embedded in a similarly wide cast.

And, to round out the set, *Ocean's Eleven* gave us Danny Ocean and Rusty Ryan (the George Clooney and Brad Pitt characters in the reboot), a set of buddies built into a caper package, then surrounded by one of those wide ensemble casts.

Interesting, right?

Buddies riff on each other. They depend on each other. They lift each other. They make each other who they are.

Putting two friends together can be great fun to watch. Think about your favorite pairings. Smile over the way they banter. Buddies are fun because watching good friends do their thing while getting into and out of trouble is always fun.

Though each character in a buddy set is independent and interesting in themselves, buddy pairings are also interesting to critique because, for purposes of story structure, the pair can be analyzed as a single entity. This allows their writers to make broader statements than they might otherwise be able to pull off.

What do I mean by that?

Well …

SOMETHING I LOVE ABOUT buddy stories is that, where stories with one main character are, by definition, about individual change first, and stories about sidekicks are stories wherein the power structure is inherently useful, the buddy story is always about collaboration, compromise, and shared values. In other words, buddy stories are about the dynamics that make up a community.

Buddy stories are, by definition, always about democracy in action.

This means the buddies represent a particular kind of community. So, a fun part of digging into buddy stories, then, is to ask yourself what communities these buddies represent, and what they mean in the context of the rest of society as depicted in the story.

Let's look at a few of my favorites.

IF YOU CANNOT LOVE *Toy Story*'s Woody and Buzz Lightyear, I feel for you.

The stories are great, the cast is amazing, and the writing is snappy and humorous. Then there are the two characters themselves, both completely adorable, if not occasionally annoying.

Hey, nobody's perfect.

Still, you'd have to be a hard person if you can't find *something* to enjoy in Buzz Lightyear and Woody.

Toy Story's buddy romp is one I particularly enjoy thinking about in terms of community and what their relationship means when extrapolated to the world I live and breathe in.

When Buzz arrives, Woody feels usurped in his role as leader of the pack. Buzz doesn't exactly yearn for control so much as he assumes it will happen simply because he is Buzz Lightyear so of course it will.

They are both good people, though, because they both want the best for everyone—a span that includes both their toy-based compatriots as well as the human beings who live in an oblivious universe above them. Toys want to enjoy good lives themselves, but they are here to serve the greater good.

In their ways, both Woody and Buzz are good leaders.

They are dynamic, loyal, smart, fearless, and dedicated. They know right from wrong.

They have flaws, though. Like all of us, they have weaknesses.

Which means they are better together than they are apart.

I suggest that the world would be a so much happier place if our politicians were all built from models like Woody and Buzz.

WHEN I FIRST THINK OF buddy stories, though, I envision the set I started this section with—Thelma and Louise, and Butch and Sundance.

They seem perfect.

I enjoyed the mechanics of their stories so much that I wrote a fantasy short ("Ties that Bind") in which a pair of enslaved gladiators struggle together to become free. It has a similar ending as Butch and Sundance, and Thelma and Louise do. In my case, since the pairing came from the gladiator pits, I was able to leave a message that was related to, but different from either of these two stories.

So, let's talk about these two buddy pairs.

LIKE MOST BUDDY PAIRS, much of the fun of *Thelma and Louise* and *Butch Cassidy and the Sundance Kid* is simply watching the buddy pair get along.

Thelma and Louise—as played by Geena Davis and Susan Sarandon—eventually get into trouble deeper than they can deal with, and the story itself depicts a harsh reality that gets more than a little dark at times. But as they experience the fullness of the world around them for the first time, their storyline comes with such intense moments of pure joy that I can't stop watching them.

Something happens, and the two smile, or laugh, then throw their heads back or wrap their arms around each other, and all is good.

Similarly, watching Paul Newman and Robert Redford play around as Butch and Sundance is a joy—one that, for me, is more satisfying than the movie itself.

Thelma and Louise and *Butch and Sundance* have similar endings structurally (both finishing as they rush to what will certainly be their deaths—he says, giving spoilers for old movies), but they leave different messages due to the way the writers put these buddies together, and what those pairings mean.

I find *Thelma and Louise* more compelling, but your mileage can vary.

My case is as follows, though.

Whereas Woody and Buzz Lightyear are fighting for a position of control within the gang of toys, Thelma and Louise are tired people, worn down by life and from having to fend off the world around them. Unlike Butch and Sundance (real-life outlaws who have had a certain kind of autonomy), at the beginning of *Thelma and Louise*, neither Thelma nor Louise has any power of their own.

No one, outside of maybe a few friends, cares about them.

Thelma is a downtrodden wife, and Louise is a waitress. They are taking a trip simply to get away from the drudgery of their lives when things go astray.

Butch and Sundance, though, begin as a pair with autonomy (they are, again, outlaws, after all). They are on a trip of their own, but that's because they are on the run from the law.

This means Butch and Sundance are *actual* bad guys. Their writers are going to have to do some trickery to get viewers to sympathize with them.

They do this by pitching Butch and Sundance as rebels fighting the system and then letting us enjoy the banter between them as they get into and out of various situations. It helps that Paul Newman and Robert Redford play them, of course. The pair are fun to watch. Still, the bottom line—even if it doesn't feel like it—is that *Butch Cassidy and the Sundance Kid* is about authorities bringing crooks to justice.

Thelma and Louise are outlaws at the end of their story, too. But it didn't start that way.

Thelma and Louise lets us watch as the world around them conspires with something akin to random chance to get them into a position where they don't have anything to lose. Or, as Thelma says to a police officer at one point: *"I swear, three days ago, neither one of us would have ever pulled a stunt like this, but if you's to ever meet my husband, you'd understand why."*

This is as good of a summary of the story as we need, and it stands as a statement of the difference between the two films.

Though Butch and Sundance are actual crooks, the writers and actors of *Butch Cassidy and the Sundance Kid* make us like the pair.

Thelma and Louise, though, are likable from the beginning of the film. As their actions get them into trouble, we get a *there but for the grace of God goes I, kind of vibe.*

Therefore, the endings—with Thelma and Louise driving off a cliff, and Butch and Sundance running into a gunfight with hundreds of law officers—though similar, feel different.

When I look at Butch and Sundance as a single entity, we see that they get into trouble because they don't want to be part of civilized society. They enjoy the life of crime—something Butch relates at one point by letting me know that Sundance will feel better once he's robbed a couple of banks. Instead of being part of society, they want, instead, to live off others and do whatever pleases them.

As fun as it is to watch Butch and Sundance, at the end of their story I know they are paying the price of justice.

They are guilty, after all.

If they are captured, they know they are going to be convicted and likely executed, so they are going to die either way.

Though also guilty of crimes, Thelma and Louise face a situation that can still feel unjust.

Even in the end, Thelma and Louise do not want to live outside of civilized society. They would like nothing more than to just be who they are and live a good, free life. Even though they've done things they now need to pay for, we see them do those things under the weight of difficult lives lived in a system that pushes them down. When Louise shoots a man, it's in defense of her friend.

If Thelma and Louise are captured, they may or may not be executed. But either way they will be locked up for a very long time. Rather than lose their newfound freedom, they are going out on their terms.

In this way, *Thelma and Louise* ends with a solid version of Live Free or Die.

AS WRITERS, we should look at buddy stories for the unique flare of their natures. When we do, we can see how the make-up of the pair together is vital to their story's resolution.

If we change the characters in the pair, we change the point of the story.

So the challenge then is for us writers to be aware of what our pairing represents, and think about what that representation means to us.

Interesting, isn't it, to see what happens when we think about a pair of characters as one entity?

Villains
Hannibal Lecter, Cruella De Vil, HAL 9000, and Beyond

Let's talk about villains, shall we? You know who I mean: those tasty bad guys who we love to hate.

Lex Luther. Darth Vader. Cersei Lannister. The Joker. Catherine Tramell from *Basic Instinct*, Gordon 'Greed Is Good' Gekko. Rachel Duncan from *Orphan Black*.

Those are some favorites, anyway.

There is always something attractive about a great villain. They appeal to the Bad Boys or Bad Girls in us. The greatest villains have it all. Charisma that oozes from their pores. Power that rides in their wake. A cold calculating brain that does things no right-minded person would ever try to pull off.

A good villain is a complex character with an ironclad background that supports their juicy nastiness. Their appearance is overwhelming the moment they arrive.

A great villain is iconic.

We cannot help but watch as they go about doing their terrible deeds of wrongness.

In *Silence of the Lambs*, for example, psychopath Hannibal Lecter—the most villainous villain of all villains—has a backstory that lets us imagine that, yes, maybe, if we were in that spot, that might be the result. Even then, Lector is so depraved that we can't fully relate to the depths of his soul.

I hope not, anyway.

But despite his coldness and cannibalism, he's got a sense of nobility around him that is hard to miss.

He is not simply a bad guy.

He is a deeply interesting bad guy with flair.

The dearly departed and deeply missed Roger Ebert wrote this in his review of the film:

"One key to the film's appeal is that audiences like Hannibal Lecter...He may be a cannibal, but as a dinner party guest he would give value for money (if he didn't eat you). He does not bore, he likes to amuse, he has his standards, and he is the smartest person in the movie."

Why is this?

What is it that makes him stand out?

How are Hannibal Lecter and all the characters in that list I just wrote down similar?

And more germane to the topic at hand, how do we—as writers—go about creating bad guys with that delicious form of gumption that appeals to readers rather than simply build bad guys who people see as speed bumps in the road that our hero needs to deal with?

Let's start here.

Different stories need different takes on the bad guy.

Cruella De Vil does not need us to dwell on any deep back-story to make her part in *101 Dalmatians* work. She's an ultra-privileged, highly pampered fashion designer with a serious supe-riority complex, and she kidnaps puppies to turn them into coats.

What else do we need to know?

Her sense of privilege and comfort with the power her posi-tion gives her informs all her actions—and is more than enough to make her real. She can be thinly drawn because we all know people who operate above their level simply because they can. Still, we love to hate Cruella because she's so firmly drawn. She's entertaining, and the limited framework of her personality is believable because, in her position within society, that frame of reference makes sense to large masses of people.

Dodie Smith, the writer of the original novel, and the Disney writers who adapted Cruella to the screen could use that frame of reference as shorthand, and be sure people got it.

Similarly, in the Cold War era, we didn't need much more than an accent and dark clothes to know that *Rocky and Bullwinkle* villains Boris and Natasha were the bad guys. I'd suggest, though, that those villains worked better in their time than they would now, at least in the US—specifically because the Cold War created an environment where that racist view—or at least highly stereotypical portrayal—was more digestible than it might be today.

Your mileage might vary, but Boris and Natasha worked as villains we love to hate for similar reasons that viewers *got* Cruella De Vil. The ubiquitous nature of the Cold War framework let writers put Boris and Natasha into stories without needing to spend any time describing who they were or why they were making Rocky and Bullwinkle's days miserable.

MOSTLY, though, as readers we want our bad guys to be stronger and more adequately motivated. It is an accepted truism that every character is the hero of their own story.

My personal experience with this came while writing my *Stealing the Sun* series, in which readers can enter with any of the first three books. Once I figured out the structure, I realized that what I had in front of me was the opportunity to delve deeply into the idea that, when in a conflict, your side is always the good guy, and the other side is always evil.

Then, of course, come the people caught in the crossfire.

For that reason, I wrote each of the first three books from the point of view of different cultures. This means I created fully realized character sets in each culture, complete with unique dreams, desires, ideals, and goals. Each culture came with social problems, and those social problems revealed heroes and villains informed by their positions around those problems.

Given the structure of these stories, there was no difference between villains and heroes when it came to their creation and portrayal.

I enjoyed creating all these characters. I enjoyed sitting in their seats and letting my thoughts and emotions swing as the story made its way through the protagonists and villains.

I'll not give direct spoilers to my work beyond saying that my dad, upon reading the first two, looked at me and said "Wow, these are really political." Which I thought was fair, even though I wasn't doing them to be directly political so much as to view situations from widely different viewpoints.

When you are dealing with galactic relations between people, and writing from multiple points of view, however, that happens.

If we are all the heroes of our own stories, then there's a reasonable chance we are also the villains of someone else's.

Therein lies another piece of magic to writing good villains, I think. Spend time in your characters' minds. Though it's impossible not to take sides, do your best not to judge them. Make them real people with real goals. Give them that glass of water as a desire, and tell me why it's important to them.

Then, if they are of evil intent, I'll have good reason to hate or fear them.

I may, in fact, even love to hate them!

I WANT to stretch our thoughts in this direction, too.

There is no need for a memorable villain to be human.

Jack London's novella "To Build a Fire" is a survival story that makes a winter storm into a villain.

HAL 9000, the ship's onboard computer, is the villain of the movie *2001: A Space Odyssey*.

HAL is a perfect psychopath—calm, cool, and collected. He's the precursor to the Borg from *Star Trek* and to *The Terminator* and Skynet. Of course, we might point out that Colossus (from *Colossus: The Forbin Project*) was the precursor to HAL 9000.

We understand HAL 9000's background because *we* made it, and that fact makes the rest of what happens as AI takes over that much more poignant.

Agent Smith from *The Matrix* has a similar flair.

Agent Smith's villainousness carries a special kind of bitterness, though. Smith is not the direct result of nature, nor is he the direct result of our own code. Agent Smith is the result of our code coding, and as such represents something even more dastardly.

Either way, though, he's simply going to work, simply executing his program. In that way, I think somewhere deep down in our veins we can all feel a connection to Agent Smith. We go to work, we do what we're expected to do, then we go home.

The true villain of *The Matrix* is the Architect, who is—like Agent Smith—a computer program, albeit one that created the whole Matrix, to begin with.

Can we get more recursive?

I don't think so.

The Alien in *Alien* is another intensely memorable non-human villain of note, more like the winter storm than a piece of AI.

Regardless, these villains are without souls as we know them. They are forces of nature, driven unwaveringly by that very nature toward a singular goal. This would not work well if the writers gave their role to a human being (unless that human was somehow broken, as in, say *Halloween*'s Michael Myers). But the idea works for these stories because the writers have shown that they aren't just being lazy and simply leaving out the rest of these villains' personalities. Instead, it's quite clear that these villains have no other personality.

Their inner drives are consistently applied in ways that are logical to the villain, and that makes the reactions and efforts of the heroes around them come off as real.

Note the hidden gem in there.

Villains become real when our heroes try everything and, because the villain reacts in ways that make sense when it comes to their natures—whatever those natures are—they fail.

So, those heroes have to try again.

Our heroes, then, become even more real as those efforts get made in ways that make sense to their own natures.

It's like a perpetual motion machine.

Hannibal Lecter is so dastardly because he is smart and because he enjoys the game. He adjusts to the moment. He's real because Thomas Harris, the writer of the original book, did intense research and built him off real serial killers. Again, to write amazing characters is to know them—even the ones who you find revolting.

The winter storm is omnipresent specifically because it cannot change.

Agent Smith creates suspense because, like the various terminators and the Alien, he is following his programming to perfection.

One gets the idea that the Architect may have more of a relationship with Hannibal Lecter than anyone would like to know.

ROGER EBERT, I think, is right about Hannibal Lecter. Readers enjoy villains. I'm no psychologist, but I figure it's fair to say that people enjoy the vicarious idea of letting themselves take big and dramatic actions, and a villain is often the ultimate example of a person who tells the world to take that long walk off the short pier.

At the very least, though, people find a good villain impossible not to watch.

Which, of course, is our goal.

Heroes
The American Film Industry
List, and Terminator

HERE'S a fun piece of information.

The American Film Industry defines a hero as "a character who prevails in extreme circumstances and dramatizes a sense of morality, courage, and purpose. Though they may be ambiguous or flawed, they often sacrifice themselves to show humanity at its best."

Per Wikipedia, here are what they consider to be the top ten heroes of all time:

1 - Atticus Finch - *To Kill a Mockingbird*

2 - Indiana Jones - *Raiders of the Lost Arc*

3 - James Bond - *Dr. No*

4 - Rick Blaine - *Casablanca*

5 - Marshal Will Kane - *High Noon*

6 - Clarice Starling - *The Silence of the Lambs*

7 - Rocky Balboa - *Rocky*

8 - Ellen Ripley - *Aliens*

9 - George Bailey *It's a Wonderful Life*

10 - T. E. Lawrence - *Lawrence of Arabia*

THEY HAVE a similar list of villains. Of interest is that one character shows up on both the AFI's hero list and their villain list. This is Arnold Schwarzenegger's Terminator, who scores the #48 spot on the list of heroes and #22 as a villain.

That's an interesting fun fact, right?

ORIGINALLY, I put this chapter before the one on Villains. But then I thought I didn't have anything to say about heroes that I haven't already covered. The AFI may have specific standards for their lists, but what is a hero if not simply a fully realized character who drives the story?

And haven't I already spent a ton of words discussing how to develop those?

Wouldn't a rehash be the slightest bit redundant?

So, I deleted my placeholder and skipped straight to Villains.

When I finished with villains, though, I realized I did have something specific to say about heroes.

While readers might want to *like* a villain, they want to *root for* a hero. I know I do. When I'm reading, I want to relate to that hero. Sometimes I want to *be* that hero.

In the villains' chapter, I noted I wrote my series *Stealing the Sun* from multiple viewpoints, and that in each section different characters from different sides were the heroes and villains. That's true. And, while I want the reader to see and understand all sides, the story itself (at least as I envision it), has a clear right side and a clear wrong side.

I suspect readers eventually root for those characters who I find the most sympathetic and see those on the other side as the villains I think they are.

I HAVE something else to say about heroes, too—something so obvious I shouldn't need to say it, but something that, even in this modern time, is still always lurking around the darker corners of the storyhood. Here it is: This need for readers to relate to and even desire to be the hero of the story is—as I noted in the chapter on physicality—why representation in fiction matters as much as it does in real life.

We should all, of course, be capable of reading about and relating to heroes of all backgrounds. But the broader the jump from me to the hero, the harder it can be for me to get there.

Writers need to understand that.

If we want our heroes to connect with people, we need to be thinking about the wide array of people coming to our books.

Think about that next time you start writing a hero.

Start by picturing the person you think is your ideal reader. Ask yourself why they'll love this character.

Then, once you think you know the answer, change that ideal reader in your mind's eye. Make them younger, or older. Swap genders. Change their races. Make them from Australia. Or if your ideal readers are from Australia, make them from India.

Whatever.

What happens when you do that?

Why do you think each of these people will love your hero?

I don't know what the right answers to these questions should be for you. I'm also not saying your story should change at all given your answers. My art is my art. Your art is your art. Your answer will be different from mine.

What I'm suggesting is that you not be blind to the situation, though.

Readers are the key to everything.

I suggest you ask the questions and think about the answers.

Then, of course, get back to work!

Archetypes
Tropes, and "Write to Market"

Until I looked it up, I always thought that the saying *That's a horse of a different color* came from *The Wizard of Oz*. Recently, I stumbled on the idea that it came from William Shakespeare. Now you know this, too.

Or at least you know I was a dummy!

Fun, right?

The things you can learn while researching books!

Anyway, in the process of thinking about villains and heroes, I've spent more time than is healthy contemplating all sorts of other archetypes that we use to develop our characters.

Depending on who you talk to, there are twelve.

Or fourteen.

Some say you need four. Others seven.

In other words, it's complicated—or at least confusing.

To be honest, I'm no longer even sure if this is a real question now.

I am beginning to think the right way to look at archetypes is to chuck all that stuff out the window and say that, for a writer, the answer is probably that there are an infinite number of archetypes.

I say that because as soon as we create a successful character, that character goes into the grist for everyone else to glom onto, twist, and duplicate in whatever fashion they can.

Of course, the hero is brave and selfless.

And the mentor is wise.

I've talked about sidekicks, supporting characters, lone-wolf heroes, and dastardly villains. I've even peeked into antiheroes.

There are damsels in distress, shamans, and witch women (both evil and wise).

A good femme fatale is always going to draw attention, so long as she also comes cloaked in an essence of danger.

There's the liar, the trickster, the everyman yearning to be free.

The outlaw.

The jester.

The loner.

Every adventure needs an explorer. Every psychological thriller needs its enigma, its innocent wayfarer, or its victim.

There are nurturers and caregivers, which may or may not be the same.

Rebels with and without causes.

Warriors.

Romantics.

See what I mean?

For every type of character, we can draw a series of unique patterns and sub-patterns, and for every one of those we can say we've created an archetype of our own.

Unless, of course, we grabbed someone else's pattern and cut our characters out of similar cloth. Still, all that means is that the archetype in question already existed.

Earlier I called Hercule Poirot, Miss Marple, and Sherlock Holmes examples of the British Gentleperson detective—which is a literary archetype. Yet, though cut from similar fabric, Poirot is different from Holmes. Just as the Robin Hood form of the outlaw is different from the Han Solo version.

One can go on.

In today's world, I often hear independently published authors talk about including tropes in their fiction—specifically around the idea of writing to market.

"I'm trying to get my tropes right," that author might say.

I ponder this.

Writers are having success with that approach right now, so who am I to argue with it? But I keep asking myself what they mean by that. In my mind, when someone says, *"You should write to market,"* I hear, *"You should understand what genre you're writing in and gear your marketing toward that genre."*

I admit I like that latter approach better, though I'm sure that's not what they mean.

I'm not here to split hairs, though.

I think we can tie the whole write-to-market concept into the idea of understanding what archetypes get people excited.

Archetypes can be tropes of their own, anyway.

They are at least related.

***

READERS LOVE CHARACTERS. And (because I haven't said it recently) since character is story, it follows reasonably that these archetypes are important for us to think about.

Fantasy readers love Frodo because he is a well-drawn everyhobbit, but science fiction folks relate just as well to Arthur Dent in *The Hitchhiker's Guide to the Galaxy*. They understand Obi-Wan Kenobi because he is the wise old man, the mentor.

Romeo is a classic romantic, but then, so is Cyrano de Bergerac.

If you need a femme fatale, do you need the Jessica Rabbit flavor, or are you in the market for *Basic Instinct*'s Catherine Tramell?

Get it right and, regardless of genre or market, the story can soar. Get it right, and, if the character is unique enough, it creates its own new archetype.

Step out of tune, though, and the story isn't going to work as well.

Redshirts
He's Dead, Jim!

WHAT DISCUSSION about characters would be complete without at least a tip of the cap to redshirts—those wonders of nature who gush up in waves from a perpetual well of cannon fodder, those minor and completely expendable folk who represent the lower-ranking members of a spaceship crew, military unit, crew of adventurers, or any other group of people who exist purely to be killed off.

In *Star Trek*, where the term originated, these characters often wore red shirts as part of their uniforms.

ASIDE: Here's a fun fact I found while researching redshirts. Of fifty-five crew members killed in Star Trek, twenty-four wore red shirts. Nine wore gold. Seven blue. That leaves fifteen unconfirmed colors.

Doing the math says that, taking only the confirmed color victims, 60% of Star Trek *deaths were of red-shirted officers.*

THOUGH SCIENCE FICTION embraced and defined the redshirt, the character type exists in all genres.

Horror relies on them in the form of the endless stream of youthful teens that your average slasher director feeds to their monsters before getting to the climax.

War movies live on redshirts.

Disaster movies eat them up like so much popcorn.

Storytellers can use redshirts for valuable purposes.

First, they serve to create a sense of danger in the story

without risking the main cast. The deaths of redshirts raise tension. They reveal how the main characters are in danger, and they help define that the stakes are high.

Redshirts can also illustrate the hierarchy within a group or organization and can help us focus on the power dynamics within the collectives that our heroes work in. Specifically, we can use redshirt deaths to help highlight the ways those deaths impact our main cast.

What does it mean, for example, if a main character doesn't react to a redshirt's death?

Or what can we do in a story when our intrepid group comes across a field of dead soldiers, and each of them deals with it in their way? How will the group change if one member is particularly hardened or callous to a redshirt's fate? Or what will it say about them if the death impacts one of our main characters so deeply that they can't go on?

Redshirts, like all non-protagonist characters, are a part of the setting, right? So how our main characters react to them is important.

In the right place, a redshirt can make an impact—even if the reader will never remember them.

Summary
Readers

HERE ARE my last thoughts on creating characters: Lighten up, Francis.

Have fun.

All the time.

As writers, when we're struggling to write them, we can serve ourselves best by stepping back and just having fun letting these characters play on the page.

Yet…

While characters entertain us, they are not here simply as song and dance folks. They are here to inspire, enlighten, and amaze us. A memorable character reflects our readers' hopes and dreams back to themselves. Sometimes these memorable characters challenge readers to question the worldviews they've built their lives around.

Characters are the clay with which we build stories.

They give those stories their heart and soul.

In the end, our character's purpose is to create a connection between the reader and the world that the story exists in.

And touching readers is the whole point of what we are doing.

Characters are the eyes through which a reader sees that story's world. They are the hearts that beat within it, and the minds that make sense of it. They are the vessel through which our readers experience the story, and as such, we should craft them with care and intention.

Of course, characters should be relatable and realistic, with flaws and strengths that make them feel like real people. They should have motivations and desires that drive the story forward.

Their actions should have consequences that ripple throughout the narrative. But only because these are things that get readers excited.

Of course, characters need to come with distinct voices and personalities that set them apart from one another. But that's because this is how readers choose their friends.

The reader is first, you see.

It's good to remember that because, while writers love the characters we create, it's the reader who will honor, cherish, and take them into themselves.

It is the reader who will celebrate them.

So, when you're writing away, and you find yourself stuck in the quagmire that is storytelling, try to just sit back, close your eyes, and think about your favorite characters from your favorite books.

Remember how they make you feel.

Think about the writer of that book as they played with those characters for the first time.

Maybe introduce those characters to your own.

Let them play together.

Enjoy.

You have come to the end of *On Creating (And Celebrating!) Characters*. If you enjoyed this book, you might like one or Ron's other explorations of the writing life:

You might also consider leaving a review at your favorite online bookseller. Even a few sentences can help!

Follow Ron!

Get updates on Ron's latest publications, and maybe even a few free books by joining!

Ron's Newsletter
http://typosphere.com/newsletter

Ron's Patreon
patreon.com/RonCollinsWrites

About Ron Collins

Ron Collins is a best-selling Science Fiction and Dark Fantasy author who writes across the spectrum of speculative fiction. With his daughter, Brigid, he edited the anthology *Face the Strange*.

His short fiction has received a Writers of the Future prize. His short story "The White Game" was nominated for the Short Mystery Fiction Society's Derringer Award.

He holds a degree in Mechanical Engineering and has worked to develop avionics systems, electronics, and information technology before chucking it all to write full-time.

Other Work by Ron Collins

<u>Novels</u>

Stealing the Sun (9 books)

Saga of the God-Touched Mage (8 books)

The PEBA Diaries (2 books)

The Knight Deception

Wakers

Fastballs and Fairies (3 Books), with Brigid Collins

Cruise Brothers Series (3 Books) with Jeff Collins

<u>Collections</u>

Collins Creek (3 volumes)

Tomorrow in All the Worlds

Picasso's Cat & Other Stories

Five Magics

Seven Days In May, with John C. Bodin

<u>Poetry</u>

Five Seven Five

<u>Nonfiction</u>

On Creating (And Celebrating!) Characters

On Being (And Becoming Again!) A Writer

List of Characters
By Book, Movie, or Show

Herein lies a register of characters that I touch on someplace in this little book—grouped here for the most part by the storylines (book, movie, or show) they were involved in. Most, of course, I've mentioned in passing so that I could accentuate a point. Those that I've given considerable attention, however, I've annotated in italic.

The length of the list surprised me, so I decided to include it here specifically to make a point.

As you scan the list, you might note characters in these stories that I didn't focus on in this book. You might think about the story these characters form, and see things differently now. Just reviewing the list might bring whole stories crashing into your mind. You might also find your mind is rushing to think through your own set of characters and your own favorite books, movies, and television shows.

This is good.

Amazing characters are all around us, right?

All we have to do is look … and love!

With that all said, here is my own character list.

To Build a Fire
A winter storm

<u>Real People</u>

Joe DiMaggio (the persona and metaphor!)
Michael Jordan (the persona and meme!)
Taylor Swift (the persona)
My buddy who plays in the bar down the road (actually fictional!)

<u>Star Trek</u>

Ro Laren
Data
The Borg

<u>Buffy & the Vampire Slayer</u>

Faith Lehane

<u>West Wing</u>

Ainsley Hayes

<u>John Wick</u>

John Wick

<u>Jack Reacher</u>

Jack Reacher

<u>James Bond</u>

James Bond

<u>Comic Book/Superhero</u>

Jessica Rabbit
Batman
Robin
The Joker
Harley Quinn
Superman/Clark Kent
Lois Lane

Jimmy Olsen
Spider-Man
Bruce Banner (Hulk)
Lex Luther

The Hunger Games
Katniss Everdeen
Prim
Their Mother

Forrest Gump
Forrest Gump
Bubba Blue
Lieutenant Dan Taylor

Die Hard
John McClane

Girl With the Dragon Tattoo (Millennium Series)
Lizbeth Salander

Little Women
Jo
Meg
Amy
Beth

Characters in Niche Short Stories
Ben
Bode Jameson

The Great Gatsby
The Great Gatsby

Jane Eyre
Jane Eyre

Aladdin
Aladdin's djinni

Lord of the Rings
Gandalf the Grey
Gollum
Gimli
Legolas

This Is Us
Jack Pearson
Rebecca Pearson
Randall Pearson

Space Odyssey 2001
HAL 9000

Colossus: The Forbin Project
Colossus

Jaws
Jaws

Silence of the Lambs
Hannibal Lecter
Clarice Starling

The Terminator
Sarah Connor
John Connor
The Terminator

Skynet

Game of Thrones
Tyrion Lannister
Brienne of Tarth
Cersei Lannister
Jaime Lannister

The Eternal Champion
Elric of Melniboné

The Umbrella Academy
Victor Hargreaves
Klaus Hargreeves
Reginald Hargreeves

The British Detective
Sherlock Holmes and Dr. Watson
Hercule Poirot
Miss Marple

Orphan Black - Clone Club
Sarah Manning
Helena
Cosima Niehaus
Alison Hendrix
Rachel Duncan
Elizabeth Childs
Katja Obinger
Veera (M.K.) Suominen
Jennifer Fitzsimmons
Krystal Goderitch
Donnie Hendrix
Felix

<u>Star Wars</u>
Yoda

Luke

Leia

Han Solo

Lando Calrissian

Darth Vadar

Obi-Wan Kenobi

<u>The Big Bang Theory</u>
Sheldon Cooper

Leonard Hofstadter

<u>Earthseed</u>
Lauren Olamina

<u>Wall Street</u>
Gordon Gekko

<u>FRIENDS</u>
Rachel Green

Chandler Bing

Monica Geller

Ross Geller

Phoebe Buffay

Joey Tribbiani

<u>Will & Grace</u>
Will

Grace

Jack

Karen

<u>Winnie the Pooh</u>

Pooh
Piglet
Eeyore
Tigger

Peanuts
Charlie Brown
Snoopy
Pig Pen

The Mary Tyler Moore Show
Mary Richards
Lou Grant
Rhoda Morgenstern
Murray Slaughter
Ted Knight
Sue Ann Nivens
Georgette Franklin
Phyllis Lindstrom

The Matrix
Agent Smith
Morpheus
Trinity
Neo
The Architect

Westworld
Teddy
Dolores
The Man in Black
Bernard
Maeve
Charlotte

Dr. Ford

Indiana Jones
Indiana Jones

Marion

A Few Good Men
Lt. Daniel Kaffee

Lt. Cdr. JoAnne Galloway

Lt. Sam Weinberg

Luther

Lt. Jonathan Kendrick

Col. Nathan Jessup

Lt. Colonel Matthew Markinson

M*A*S*H
Trapper John McIntyre

BJ Hunnicutt

Colonel Harry Potter

Frank Burns

Margaret "Hot Lips" Hoolihan

Colonel Henry Blake

Radar O'Reilly

Klinger

Father Mulcahy

Major Charles Emerson Winchester III

Saga of the God-Touched Mage
Darien

Garrick

Stealing the Sun
Torrance Black

<u>The Goldfinch</u>
Theo Decker

<u>Perry Mason</u>
Perry Mason
Della Street

<u>Xena: Warrior Princess</u>
Xena
Gabrielle

<u>Calvin & Hobbes</u>
Calvin
Hobbes

<u>Thelma and Louise</u>
Thelma
Louise

<u>Butch Cassidy and the Sundance Kid</u>
Butch Cassidy
The Sundance Kid

<u>Shrek</u>
Shrek
Donkey

<u>Toy Story</u>
Woody
Buzz Lightyear

<u>Ocean's Eleven</u>
Danny Ocean
Rusty Ryan

<u>Basic Instinct</u>
Catherine Tramell

<u>101 Dalmatians</u>
Cruella De Vil

<u>Rocky & Bullwinkle</u>
Boris
Natasha
Rocky
Bullwinkle

<u>Aliens</u>
The Alien
Ellen Ripley

<u>Halloween</u>
Michael Myers

<u>To Kill A Mockingbird</u>
Atticus Finch

<u>Casablanca</u>
Rick Blaine

<u>High Noon</u>
Marshal Will Kane

<u>Rocky</u>
Rocky Balboa

<u>It's a Wonderful Life</u>
George Bailey

Lawrence of Arabia

T. E. Lawrence

The Hitchhiker's Guide to the Galaxy

Arthur Dent

Romeo and Juliette

Romeo

Cyrano de Bergerac

Cyrano de Bergerac